T0354681

CARE
for Your Clients

CARE
for Your Clients

Three Steps to Building a Great Brand
Around Client Experience

David S. Harrison

ARCHWAY
PUBLISHING

Archway Publishing books may be ordered through booksellers or by contacting:

Archway Publishing
1663 Liberty Drive
Bloomington, IN 47403
www.archwaypublishing.com
844-669-3957

ISBN: 978-1-6657-6705-7 (sc)
ISBN: 978-1-6657-6706-4 (hc)
ISBN: 978-1-6657-6707-1 (e)

Library of Congress Control Number: 2024921483

Print information available on the last page.

Archway Publishing rev. date: 10/30/2024

To Wilhe, Mateo, Diego, and Rainer.
May you continue to make the world a brighter place.

INTRODUCTION

Saturday morning. My usual thing is a fifty-mile bike ride with Ryan starting at 6:00 a.m. Start early, finish early. We rode our typical route, and at mile ten, we hit the northernmost point of our ride at the Ocean Institute. I reached down to grab my water bottle for a drink of electrolyte-infused water, and to my surprise and dismay (and maybe even horror), I found that I had forgotten both of my water bottles in my rush to get out of the house.

Endurance exercise requires rehydration. There is no way I can go fifty miles on a road bike without some water and probably some level of electrolytes as well. No problem; there's a convenience store at North Beach. Five miles, fifteen to twenty minutes of riding, and I'll pop in to said convenience store and grab some kind of "ade."

We ride up to the store. I hop off my bike and run (well, maybe walk quickly) in. At the refrigerated section of sports drinks, there are multiple options. I pick one and walk up to the counter. It's 7:00 a.m., and there are only two people in this store—me and the dude who is working behind the counter. As I stand there, trying to pay, I see that the individual running the store that morning is pulling some type of food product out of an oven and putting these products on a tray, ultimately to go into a display case on the counter. He's wearing unfitted cellophane food-service-type gloves (think 1970s cafeteria-lady-style gloves with four, not five, fingers) and carefully going about his task at hand (pun intended), all the while completely ignoring me.

There is no way, I say to myself, that he could not be aware of my presence. Not looking, not nodding, not telling me he'll be with me in a minute. He was either hyper-focused, very shy, ridiculously rude, or just being a typical clerk in a convenience store. It is a convenience store after all.

Not wanting to be rude but also wanting to get on with this transaction and get back to my bike ride, I decided to confirm my presence with a loud "ahem." This is, to my knowledge, known through most of the civilized world as an audible attention getter. The obnoxious noise did nothing, and there was still no acknowledgment of my existence following both the first and second time I cleared my throat in an attempt to get his attention.

Yes, ultimately, he completed his task, walked two steps to where I was standing at the counter, wordlessly scanned my item, and watched me use Apple Pay to complete the transaction. And then Ryan and I were off to complete our ride. The totality of this transaction was less than five minutes—probably less than three minutes. The convenience store was conveniently located, as I had already known. It was, as I had expected, conveniently stocked with multiple variations of products that suited my needs that morning. It was inarguably convenient, notwithstanding the unnecessary length of the stop that seemed to be of concern to only one person on the planet—me.

It was convenient even in the absence of conversation or courtesy. It was convenient even though it had only the most basic level of service. I was able to pay for a product using my phone. It was convenient because that is the brand of a convenience store. And I think it is safe to say that Mr. Convenience Store Man's personal brand had no link to the brand of that convenience store on this particular Saturday morning. He was just there to enable the transaction. It could have been a robot.

My attention was less focused on the fact that I had met my hydration needs and more so on why the transaction seemed like a lost opportunity for the proprietor of this store. It simply got me thinking about retail businesses that have any type of service component. Why didn't the person working in the store acknowledge me? They didn't even say hello. Do they need to? Is service a part of the convenience store experience at any level? Will I come back? Will kindness, acknowledgment, or maybe even a suggestion on a better-value "ade" drink make a difference for me? The value proposition of the convenience store is, in its most basic formulation, convenience, and I got what I needed—so they delivered.

It was an experience. A weird experience, to be sure, but definitely a memorable experience. I remembered it well enough that, after a fifty-mile bike ride that included a stop for coffee, I was able to write down the play-by-play when I got home.

The opportunity to create a positive experience exists in every interaction with a potential customer or client. A business has, in these interactions, an opportunity to be kind, to be helpful, or to simply acknowledge the existence of a customer, and these opportunities can serve as a differentiator for some retailers.

Nordstrom has, and continues to have, a very well-earned reputation for outstanding customer service. You expect outstanding customer service in a Nordstrom, as this is part of their brand, and in my experience, I have received outstanding customer service every time I have shopped in a Nordstrom store. Their staff provide this service, not the store managers or the Nordstrom family; it's the employees on the front lines who make customer service happen at Nordstrom.

And I know that this is from the Department of Redundancy Department: every interaction with a customer is an opportunity. "An opportunity for what?" you may ask. It's an opportunity to build and reinforce your brand around customer service, as in a Nordstrom store. Even further, it's an opportunity to create positive, differentiated customer experience that engenders brand loyalty and leads customers to prefer your brand over your competitors. Positive brand differentiation and customer loyalty—those sound pretty good!

Customer service is a differentiator for many brands. As an example, Amazon and Costco make returning products very easy. That's a part of service, and it differentiates these companies from some of their competitors.

Great customer service is important, but it's more important when it is part of an overall customer interaction that leads to a positive customer experience. Customer service per se is not sufficient to create lasting, differentiated customer experience. Experience is more than just customer service, as we'll explore in this book.

Positive customer experience is the real differentiator, driven, in part, by service. Experience exists in the many small things and occasional large things that your employees do for your customers. It can, and should, be part of every customer interaction. Many companies seem to understand this.

- You can go into an Apple store, and someone will kindly and patiently guide you through all the iPhone options so you can make a studied decision as to the model that works best for you.
- The checkout person at Trader Joe's always offers a compliment on my purchases or asks me what I plan to do with all the candy, crackers, beer, and wine that I am purchasing!
- The very nice teenager taking my order in the car line at Chick-Fil-A always says, "My pleasure."
- The person taking my order at my neighborhood Starbucks will brew a fresh batch of blonde roast for me, while the Starbucks guy at the Orange County Airport will move so fast he looks like a movie special effect, but I appreciate that he's keeping the line moving as fast as possible (and he always gets my order right!).
- Car dealers tell you in their advertising that they have the best service.
- Airlines will advertise that they have a better client experience.

The businesses noted above are manufacturers, retailers, and service providers. They all try to create a better customer experience.

Can customer experience be a differentiator for all retailers? Of course it can. Some retail establishments are about convenience (exhibit 1 in this category is noted above), and others may be about having the lowest price. Even these have the potential to differentiate their businesses on great client experience.

One thing before we dive into this is to talk about customers and clients. Here are two definitions from the *Merriam-Webster Dictionary* app:

Customer: one who purchases a commodity or service.
Client: a person who engages the professional advice or
services of another.

Both are about purchasing. A customer buys stuff or services. A client buys professional services from organizations that may also offer (for a price) professional advice. For our purposes, I'm going to use the term *client* throughout the book. I was certainly not a client of the convenience store mentioned earlier. Perhaps a mindset by the clerk working in that store that considers each customer to actually be a client would have changed the way that the clerk interacted with me. It's possible that such an interaction could have made me a raving fan of the store. Going forward, we'll use the word *client* as we discuss client experience as a differentiator.

Are there any specific aspects of client experience that are important elements of a retail transaction at a convenience store? Clearly not, if you were to ask most convenience store owners. Should they be? Should the small details of how you treat a customer, or potential customer, inside your retail establishment be important?

Should client experience be an integral part of the retail experience, and can it be a differentiator in the retail world?

The answer is yes. The reason is to positively differentiate your brand to make it the preferred retailer, convenience store, or discount store. There's competition out there. How can you beat them? What will create brand loyalty with your clientele? A better client experience can make the difference. It can evoke, in your clients and potential clients, a positive emotional response that preferentially moves them to your store, product, or service.

Are the client experience components of retail establishments the same as the client experience components of professional services? Yes and no. An example is the ease of returns. You bring something back to a retailer that emphasizes this element of service; the customer experience element is *how* they take care of you. This is where your company's employees interact with clients, and this interaction is the "client experience." In fact, any interaction between an employee and a client, whether online, in person, in a telephone conversation, or text messaging, is an opportunity to create a better client experience. It's an opportunity to create differentiation. It's an opportunity to make your brand stand out above your competitors.

Let's agree that client experience is an important element of brand differentiation for both retail and services businesses and that it can be a significant positive differentiator for your business if done right. How then does one do customer experience right? Is there a formula for providing great service that transcends the type of business? Is there a client experience formula that might elevate a convenience store, differentiate a retail establishment, or keep clients in your professional services fold? I think there is.

There is a way (and I know I just said this, but I want to say it again) to make great client experience part of your brand and make that experience something that will positively differentiate you from your competitors. That is what I want to explore in this book.

This book is anecdotal, not academic research. It is based on my experience serving in various marketing, sales, and client account management leadership roles in a large engineering and construction company. It is also based on my experience as someone who consumes products and services. I think about experience everywhere I go—in the grocery store, at the doctor's office, getting a beer with my buddies, sitting in church (I should be paying attention to other stuff; I'm deeply aware of that), or listening to a music streaming service. I'm always asking how the experience in that retail establishment or service organization could be better.

My path in the world of client service started accidentally. I was serving in a regional operations management role when I was asked to improve the overall level of service that we provided our clients. That's a pretty vague remit, and I really didn't know what it meant (neither did my boss, as it turns out). I took the job because I wanted to do something new, but I wanted to know more about what he was thinking. He told me that the CEO thought that we could differentiate ourselves by being more "personable" (the CEO's word) and friendly than our competitors. I said yes. It sounded like an interesting challenge.

They were thinking service, and I soon learned that it wasn't really about service; it was about client experience. I embarked on my own research into the specifics of great client experience and adapted some things that I had learned in business classes at UCLA and a week-long course at Harvard centered around leading professional services firms. I read books and articles in *Harvard Business Review, Bloomberg BusinessWeek*, and many other publications with a focus on client service. There are some experts out there like David Maister, whose research and books provide tremendous insights for the marketing of professional services. Others, like Joe Pine, focus on the value of client experience.

Friends and family will tell you that I talk about client experience a lot—probably too much. Abraham Maslow once said, "If all you have is a hammer, everything looks like a nail." This applies to me with respect to client experience; I think about it in every transaction, from the convenience store (as previously noted) on up to a visit to the doctor's office. I am obsessed with client experience, and this leads to my friends and family members feeling free to share their client experience stories (both good and bad) with me on a regular basis.

I'm always wondering how it could be done better. As a practicing engineer, I constantly asked my clients about service and client experience. Did they like the service they received? What specific aspects did they like? Can they define a preferred experience with a service provider? What would they like for the service provider to do differently?

As a consumer, I also ask employees at service and retail establishments that I frequent about great service. What training did you receive? What do you think are the elements of great service? Do you think that this is a differentiator for your company? How would you do it better? You get the idea.

I offer a formula that works for services marketing and that I believe will work across this wide spectrum of services and retail marketing. This formula is inspired by all those who provided great service to me— and by a nonverbal dude in a convenience store.

The first big question is "What is great experience?" You may have an amazing experience at a retail establishment or with a service provider. This experience may lead you to highly value that brand. Amazing experiences are rare; more often, it's the many small things that go into interactions between a business organization and a client.

Client experience is client defined. Your employee interacts with them to find out what they are about and then works to make sure they deliver to meet the client's needs. Client experience can also be little things that you know will be appreciated by your client. The reason you know this is that your experience, or the experience of others in your organization, tells you that clients appreciate the "little things."

I found that developing a communication flow with my clients that met their personality and needs was something they valued. Communication methods and styles over the course of a six-month project often did not occur to my clients at the outset of a project. Your employees' work experience can serve to enhance your client's experience.

As part of my new job, I started observing my company's best "service providers." I'm a big believer in observation. You have to be at the front lines to really know, in an unadulterated manner, what's going on. The top *client service managers* were assigned to me. Other companies might call these individuals account executives, or senior account executives, or some variation on this theme.

Seeing is believing. I started asking our top client service managers if I could tag along with them to visit their clients. All said yes, but very few of them actually visited their clients on a regular basis. Most simply relied on emails, texts, and phone conversations when engaging their clients.

One of the client service managers, Fred, took me to visit one of his clients in the Northeast US. Fred had clearly communicated with them that he was bringing someone along, so they were expecting Fred and his "boss." He knew almost everyone in the building and introduced me to everyone we encountered. He was polite, friendly, and very well known in this particular facility. We had a big project opportunity coming up with this client, and Fred was asking questions about this so that we could be responsive when putting together a proposal to do this work.

Other client service managers gave me a schedule for a visit six months in the future, and there were some who told me that it was a big hassle to visit their client, so they didn't do it very often. Over the next twelve months, I watched these individuals in action. I saw how they prepared for client meetings, how they interacted with their clients, and how the clients responded to them. We discussed client experience, and I watched them chip away at trying to create a better experience for their clients.

I had my own clients as well, and I started to develop my client service ethos and apply it to these clients. I engaged former clients and asked them about client service and how that may have been a differentiator for them in the procurement of engineering and construction services from my company.

I didn't, however, focus solely on my own business and clients to develop my formula for client experience. I started to pay attention to interactions that I was having in coffee shops or retail establishments. How was I treated when I bought that cup of coffee or was searching for a pair of shoes? What were the interactions like? How did the person working in the coffee shop, or the shoe department, respond to my questions? Were there any after-sale interactions, and how valuable were these?

One thing I noticed is that there is a wide gulf between retailers that try to provide service and those that are focused on other aspects of differentiation, such as price. That probably has to do with the fact that some retailers are focused on other things like low prices, keeping their shelves stocked, or having a lot of options in their stores. I also noticed that some retail establishments do service really well. They have helpful staff and easy return policies. They answer the phone when you call and strive to help you without having you wait on hold through twenty minutes of soft jazz. They successfully combine products and service in a way that positively differentiates them from their competitors. And isn't that the goal for most of us? To be positively differentiated from our competition.

All of this factored into what I thought made for great client experience. I went through several iterations of my formula before I settled on one that I think makes sense for both retail and service business.

This formula has three key components. The first is focused on why client experience can be a differentiator. This is a discussion of consumer purchasing behavior, branding, and a concept called *brand convergence*. This concept posits that the convergence between the stated corporate brand image and the personal brands of the employees enhances the overall brand of the organization.

The second component is called CARE. It's an acronym for an overarching philosophy around client interaction. In plain language, it's a way you treat your clients. We will describe each element of CARE, discuss why this might be a critical element of client service, and provide some examples. That will get us through what to do and provide some thoughts on ways you may actually start doing these things.

Finally, the third component offers some suggestions for building a brand convergent team that CAREs for your clients. This is based on my experience and the experience of successful companies that have figured out how to implement the concept of CARE in their business and drive brand convergence. This will give you some ideas on what it takes to actually implement brand convergent behavior within your business.

There are companies that get this right. Examples are offered throughout the book. When it's a positive example, I'll give real names of organizations and, in some cases, real names of the people involved. For negative examples, I'll provide some anonymity, especially for individuals. I'm not trying to hurt any person or any company; sometimes good people have bad days.

Here is a positive example of a company that seems to understand and practice the concept of providing great client experience. Southwest Airlines consistently scores very high in customer surveys like the J.D. Power North America Airline Satisfaction Survey. What do they do to earn this consistently high rating? Southwest has a brand built around experience, and they have employees who understand this and want to help make the flying experience as good as it can possibly be. That's brand convergence. Both the company and their employees embody CARE. They operate in a timely manner, communicate clearly, and pay attention to customers.

Southwest employees do all they can to be kind to passengers. Southwest (and other highly rated airlines) invest in recruiting people who can embody their brand and training their staff to find ways to make the passenger experience better.

You may have been a passenger on a Southwest flight where the flight attendants sang "Happy Birthday" to a passenger or offered the obligatory safety announcements in the genre of a stand-up comedy routine. My favorite experience was watching Southwest flight attendants celebrating a very inebriated couple's engagement on the 7:00 a.m. flight from Burbank to Las Vegas. It seemed that the man had popped the question to his fiancée either in the airport lounge or when they got on the plane. My only evidence for this is that the fiancée was crying, with her mascara running down her face in what I can only call Goth-rocker style. Nevertheless, the couple seemed very happy, their friends on the flight were clearly delighted, and the flight attendants were enjoying substituting beer for champagne to help the couple celebrate.

Southwest strives for the two things that every airline passenger wants: 1) getting themselves and their luggage to their location safely; and 2) being on time. They add a great experience on top of that, and that experience becomes the differentiator.

That's it. It seems pretty simple, but it is very hard to do. In fact, it's so hard to execute that I believe this quote from Shakespeare's *The Merchant of Venice* perfectly applies:

> If to do were as easy as to know what were good to do, chapels had been churches and poor men's cottages princes palaces. It is a good divine that follows his own instructions: I can easier teach twenty what were good to be done, than be one of the twenty to follow my own teaching.

There are a lot of things that are good to do yet very hard to do. Cleaning your house is an example. Having a clean home is good, but doing it is hard. Saving money for retirement is also something that's good to do yet hard to do. Treating people nicely when you are having a bad day … I think Shakespeare got this right.

Let's do both in this book. Let's figure it out (the easy part) what great client experience might mean, and let's talk about doing (the hard part).

CHAPTER ONE

Brand Convergence

Why Client Experience Is a Brand Differentiator

The first step in the process of creating a brand around great client experience is brand convergence. This occurs when your corporate brand and the personal brands of your client-facing employees converge—when they are the same. This creates a powerful synergy for companies that wish to be branded around great client experience. It fosters client loyalty, and it can positively drive the performance of your organization. The concept of brand convergence provides a mechanism for demonstrating to your employees the value of a client experience–oriented brand and showing them their very important role in developing and maintaining this brand.

The executive director of a large municipal government transportation agency in New Zealand, when asked what came to mind when he thought of the brand of a specific engineering consultant, replied, "It's the people." That was his simple reply. The terms *quality, cost, responsiveness, value, innovation, technical expertise, excellence*—and there are so many more—did not come to mind. Simply, he said it's the people that the engineering consultant provides—and the things that these people do (and he said a lot more about this)—that come to mind when he thinks about an engineering consultant's brand.

1

The brand. Your personal brand. The company's brand.

The key concepts that are repeated in virtually every definition of the term *corporate brand* are product/service identification and differentiation. The term *personal brand* is generally never included in a description of corporate brand. Perhaps it is assumed that employees will embody the corporate brand. That's a bad assumption. There are tremendous synergies between personal brand and corporate brand in the world of professional services. Those synergies include such differentiable brand elements as technical reputation, specific related experience, positive client references, and client experience. If you ask the clients, it's pretty tough to tell who is better on a technical basis. Ask them about experience, and they have a much easier time telling you which firm they prefer to work with.

The term *brand* has different connotations within the framework of the market sector or industry for which it is employed. In the world of consumer products, branding might be represented by the reliability and consistency of a product *and* can also include the feel or vibe of the product. In other words, brands are perceived both objectively and subjectively. Toothpaste, light bulbs, and automobiles are branded. You generally purchase these products for objective reasons: the things you believe (or the packaging tells you to believe) they can do for you. You may purchase based on price if you believe all other variables are equal, but for some items, like toothpaste, price is normally irrelevant. You may purchase toothpaste because you like the way it tastes, light bulbs because you think they will last longer, or a car because you can drive it more safely in the snow. You may purchase these products because of their logo (you may like the logo, or it may remind you that you know about this particular company) or because you like the color scheme on the packaging.

There are cases where branding is less about customers and clients and more about employees. Ford Motor Company once famously had a marketing campaign where they stated that for Ford, "Quality is job number one." One could deduce from this that Ford wanted you to believe that their brand was all about quality. Ford was also aiming this at the many employees of Ford Motor Company, their Ford Dealer network, and their multitude of suppliers, reminding them that quality was job number one for everyone who touched a car during the assembly, transportation, delivery, and repair processes for Ford vehicles.

Companies have logos, color palettes, and taglines that are a big part of their marketing and branding. Many companies focus on these elements of branding, forgetting that the ultimate goal of branding is to evoke a positive emotional reaction in the mind of the consumer. One may ask how successful color schemes and logos are in achieving this goal. I submit that some are highly successful. I've been lectured on the benefits and value of Nike products by a seven-year-old boy. Nike would be pleased to know that this entire three-minute soliloquy on the greatness that is Nike was inspired solely by the young lad seeing the Nike swoosh on a store. That's all it took to unleash the positive feelings that this young Nike fan had for the brand. That is a successful brand.

If your logo can do that, you are in rare company with Nike, Apple, Lululemon, Tesla, and the Major League Baseball team that you have been cheering for since you were a nine-year-old. If your logo and tagline don't get that kind of reaction, wouldn't you like to find a way for someone to get all hyped up about your products (and maybe even service)? Don't you want to have raving fans who wear clothes and caps with your logo, go out of their way to frequent your place of business, and tell everyone about the greatness (and "beauty," if my seven-year-old friend is to be believed about Nike) and trustworthiness of your company? Of course you want this. Everyone wants this; even the convenience store operators would like to have raving fans.

This can be taken one step further for some products like computers or smartphones. Apple makes both, and some consumers prefer Apple products for objective reasons. They certainly aren't the least expensive. Most people don't have the technical skills to actually determine that an Apple product is technically better than a competitive product. You may believe this deep in your soul, but you would have a hard time arguing for your presumption of superiority with anyone who is a computer engineer.

You may have purchased your Apple product for any number of objective or subjective reasons: to be consistent with your teenage child, everyone else has one, reliability, feel, or ease of use. You most likely felt it was simply a better product than its competitors. This is the subjective *feel* or *vibe* of a product that is equally important, if not more important, to a brand image than the objective features or elements of the product.

If you purchased that product at an Apple store, you also got the *experience*, which is another strong facet of the Apple brand (more about this later). Again, your value system must intersect with the product's brand. If you value "cool" and "easy to use," you are likely strongly considering an Apple product.

Branding is intended to differentiate. The toothpaste makes your teeth whiter. The iPhone is easy to use and cool. The flat-screen TV has more features. Branding can tell you what a product does or how it is different from the competition.

One significant manner in which consumer products are branded is advertising. Print and electronic media advertising feeds the iPhone cool factor and the Prius green factor. This isn't the only way brands are promoted. Having the right influencers and celebrity endorsers can also go a long way to evoke a positive feeling for a brand. People like Shaquille O'Neal and Jennifer Garner lend their names and images to many different brands, with very positive effects for those brands.

People are a big part of branding in both a positive and negative way. Famous individuals with outstanding "Q-scores" can enhance the way a client sees a brand and create the positive response that marketers are looking for. They can also do a lot of damage. There have been many instances where a powerful, well-regarded brand representative with an amazing Q-score can cause havoc within a marketing department. What happens when your brand spokesperson or influencer says something that 99 percent of the world feels is inappropriate or wrong, gets caught cheating in an athletic endeavor, or gets raided by the FBI? I don't need to tell you who these people are, but you could ask a marketing executive at Jell-O, Trek Bicycles, the US Postal Service, Nike, Subway, Adidas, Ciroc Vodka, and many others what it was like to find out that their beloved spokesperson had some major issues. Subway had built an entire marketing campaign that lasted for many years around a spokesperson who turned out to be a pedophile. That will take you to marketing DEFCON 1 in a hurry.

Companies have brands. People have brands. If they work together, wouldn't that be a net positive for your brand? Is it possible that corporate and personal brands that work together could be synergistic with respect to the promotion of a brand and the ability of that brand to create clients who are raving fans? You know that I'm going to say yes to both of these questions.

Just as a reminder. A corporate brand is intended, among other things, to evoke a positive emotional reaction in the mind of your company's clients and potential clients. There are many brands that do this successfully. REI is a retailer that has a strong, positive brand.

People go to REI to get outdoor gear and to get advice from the REI salespeople who, in most cases, really seem to know what they are talking about. When you feel that you got a good deal, that you purchased a product that you will be able to use in the way it is intended and in the way you need it to work, then you have a positive reaction. When the REI salesperson is knowledgeable and friendly and takes the time to understand what you really need, then you have a positive experience.

Corporate Brands

All of us have a pretty good sense of corporate brands. Many times, a company will just tell us what their brand is through their tagline, packaging, advertising, or other promotional activities. Red Bull "gives you wiiiings." It's an energy drink. Nike wants you to "just do it." Get out there and use those shoes, athletic wear, or other Nike-branded merchandise. Subaru wants you to know that their cars are all about love. If you love your family and want to protect them, you'll put your sixteen-year-old child in your used Subaru and buy a new one for yourself.

Red Bull is about energy—the type of energy one gets from an energy drink. What would happen if Red Bull featured a lethargic, lazy person in one of their ads? Such a person couldn't get wings from Red

Bull or perhaps any other energy drink on the planet. If Nike sponsored office workers instead of professional basketball players, would this help their branding and shoe sales? (I know that in some major cities, like Chicago, the office workers wear their sneakers onto the train and walking to their office, so maybe sponsoring office workers could work for Nike in some target markets). If Subarus didn't have the highest level of crash rating, would they still be about love?

Corporate brands need to be consistent with the performance of their products. Wherever there is an interface between a client and a representative of the company, there should also be consistency. If you are working to differentiate your company by making these interactions better, or providing a higher level of service, then you need to figure out how to get every client-facing person and every client-engaging process in your company working to fit with this brand. It's that simple, and it's that hard.

Branding in professional services firms is simply not the same as consumer products branding. In the services arena, perceptions of reliability, consistency, quality, and product integrity are not rolled off an assembly line; rather, they are highly customized, and the clients all possess varied definitions of reliability, consistency, and integrity. Nevertheless, brand plays a role in the minds of the clients in these transactions, but it is much more highly related to the people who are engaging with the client. I refer you to the public transportation agency executive who addressed some executives from my company as noted at the start of this chapter. As a reminder, he said that he buys services based on the people providing the service, not the company per se.

These same concepts apply to the experience element of a potential client who visits a retail establishment to buy a product. They are purchasing a product; that is the baseline truth. They may, however, also value reliability, consistency, and integrity. They want to trust that they will get the best experience along with a great product. Clients of service companies don't always think about experience. They do, however, recognize a great experience as well as a terrible experience, and both of these can drive future decision-making about where they will go for services.

Your corporate brand of a better client experience is a bold statement. Many companies successfully operate in this realm. Nordstrom really does seem to have excellent service. They aren't the only ones. Carmax is another company whose brand seems to be about client experience.

Carmax? Really? Yup. I was considering selling a car, and they treated me very respectfully, explained their process to me, gave me a time frame for putting the offer together, and then delivered five minutes early. Of course, I was disappointed that the offer seemed low (so I kept the car), and I was also a bit perturbed that the appraiser had moved the driver's seat really far back (it's just a pet peeve of mine; the appraiser would have no idea that this bothered me).

One would think that Carmax is more about selling cars to people than buying cars from people. Their taglines are "The way car buying should be" and "A hassle-free kind of happy." The second could be construed to refer to the selling process.

There were dozens of people in Carmax on that Tuesday morning trying to sell their car and almost nobody on the car lot looking for cars. It seems that Carmax purchasing cars from people is a big part of what they do. I did not sell my car that day, but in the fifty-five minutes or so that I spent waiting to complete the appraisal process with nothing else to do, I wandered the Carmax lot and wondered why I hadn't gone there to purchase the used, late-model, fire engine–red Corvette that they had sitting on their lot in lieu of my SUV that I was sort of happy with.

Carmax, in reality, is about service. They want you to know that things are hassle-free. The Carmax customer-facing person, Mary Jane, was very kind, thorough, efficient, friendly, and accurate with respect to the timing of the process. In fact, as she was just getting my information, a disgruntled customer interrupted her and told her that she was promised that she'd be next to be helped. (I had an appointment; the disgruntled and irritated person did not.) Mary Jane was very kind and simply said, "I will help you next after this person," and that took care of things. I should also note that I interacted with only Mary Jane. I didn't meet the appraiser, but I do know that he (or she) is likely to be a very tall human being, considering the location of the driver's seat.

Overall, it was a hassle-free experience, and even though I didn't leave happy that I'd been able to sell my car for top dollar, I didn't leave unhappy either. Carmax is a service company, and they provided a really good experience that left me with a positive, if slightly unfulfilled, feeling. The Carmax hassle-free brand matched my specific reality on that day.

Personal Brands

You already know lots of people who live and die with their personal brand. It's something that is frequently used by people who are celebrities, people whose *brand* is part of their public identity. Many business executives have a personal brand. CEOs want to be known as caring, tough, successful, charitable, or whatever other adjectives work for them. Many actors, musicians, and athletes have personal brands that are used to create large, sustainable business empires. Politicians have them too, but I don't want to go that far in this book. If you need more information on the personal brand of any politician, you can get it from a multitude of basic cable channels.

At Carmax, Mary Jane seemed to have a personal brand of service, caring, and efficiency. Let's talk a bit more about personal brand with respect to interactions with business clients. The starting point should be the massive quantity of literature out there about personal brands.

It's all a matter of perception. Beauty, or in this case, brand, is in the eye of the beholder. The brand of a company, an individual, a nonprofit organization, a product, or service is simply what the consumer, purchaser, donor feels and believes about the products or services produced by the individual or organization.

This is true of a personal brand. What do others believe about you? Tom Peters wrote an article about personal branding that was published in 1997 in *Fast Company* titled "The Brand Called You." OK, fair enough, he gets the credit. You can read about personal brand in just about any business magazine.

Your personal brand is effectively and essentially communicated through your interactions with your clients. You will communicate your personal brand very quickly in a business interaction by what you do *and* what you say. You can't tell someone you care; you have to show it. Theodore Roosevelt, who was the twenty-sixth president of the United States, said, "No one cares how much you know until they know how much you care." Do you think this is true? It probably isn't for my convenience store friend, but if you're buying a car, or trying to sort through a phalanx of alternatives, it's very true.

My company had a longstanding client that I'll simply call "Client." We did multiple projects for this client at any given time, and one of my colleagues, who I'll call Henry, was working on a project for Client. Henry was telling me one morning about a very important upcoming meeting with Client's chief engineer scheduled for that very afternoon. Henry was prepared, and he left about fifteen minutes early to make the forty-five-minute drive to Client's offices. I didn't expect to see Henry back in the office until the following day, but in the middle of the afternoon, he was back in the office, lolling around in his cubicle with his feet up on his desk.

I asked him about his meeting with the chief engineer, who had a reputation (actually, it was really this guy's personal brand) of asking tough questions and demanding excellence from service providers. "Didn't happen," Henry told me. I asked what happened. "I got there early and then waited until about twenty minutes after our scheduled meeting time, and he was tied up in some other stuff, so I left." My company is a service provider. If a client wants to make you wait to meet with them or provide services, that is their prerogative.

Looking back on this, I knew Henry to be a bit temperamental and also a bit arrogant. How did I know that? It was how he behaved with his colleagues. So, it should be no surprise that this is how he behaved with a client who was late to a meeting. Arrogance and intolerance are not two things that anyone wants to be known for. It certainly was not what we, as a company, wanted to be known for. Shortly after this incident, my colleague Henry became a former colleague; we were fortunately able to keep the client.

What was Henry doing in a consulting engineering practice? He did not have the right temperament for this and probably should not have been in a client-facing role. Not everyone is cut out to successfully engage with clients, much less difficult and demanding clients. Some just don't have the right personal brand for a service business or for any business where client interaction is required.

The Apple store is an example of the opposite end of the personal brand spectrum. Our laptop seemed to have died after the watery contents of a thirty-ounce Stanley tumbler were accidently discharged directly into the keyboard. We determined that, if we were lucky, the laptop was merely in an Apple coma and perhaps could be revived by someone with more technical skills and knowledge, so we made an appointment with the Genius folks at Apple for service.

The Apple employee greeted us in a friendly manner and immediately sprang into action to attempt a life-saving action for our eight-year-old laptop. At the same time, he was trying to help a very grumpy and mean-spirited individual sitting next to us who did not have an appointment but seemed to be upset with this employee's inability to do whatever computer alchemy they thought should be done. The Apple employee was kind but firm. He couldn't do magic for this very unhappy person. I decided to cheer him up by getting him into a conversation.

The first thing I did was ask him about his watch. It was a decent Swiss watch, and I usually notice unusual watches. He told me that his girlfriend had given this to him as a gift, and he also told me that he didn't like wearing an Apple watch because he preferred to use his phone, and now he had a nice Swiss watch that he also preferred to wear. That's an honest response. I decided to ask him about the grumpy customer who had just left. Specifically, I asked him about any training he may have received to deal with difficult people. His answer was surprising. "Very little," he told me.

Dealing with difficult people is difficult. I asked him how he knew how to handle this individual in a professional manner. He told me that, in his opinion, Apple hired people with high emotional intelligence, gave them some basic interpersonal communication training, and supplemented this with lots of technology training. He'd also been working at Apple for several years and had "seen it all." This wasn't the first grumpy person whose electronic device was unfixable or whose problem was unsolvable. The best he could do was to be patient and kind. That makes a lot of sense.

Apple wants us to "think differently." The whole vibe of an Apple store is about cool technology and lots of new technology that they are constantly bringing out. They offer technology that they want people to use to enhance their lives. If you are a technology noob, they'll take the time to explain stuff to you. If you are a technical expert, they'll stand by and answer your questions if you have any. They'll let you freely play with any device that is on display, including their new (at this time, they were new) virtual reality Vision Pro headset. This seems very consistent with their brand. I really appreciated my conversation with the Apple employee and was grateful for his efforts to revive our now officially proclaimed dead laptop.

We asked him a few questions about new laptops. He asked us some good questions about how we use the computer, and we walked away with a new laptop. His personal brand fit right into Apple's corporate brand. They sold a new product, and we were satisfied customers.

Just a few more thoughts on personal brands, brought to you by any search engine that can find stuff on the internet.

Harvard Business Review is a good source for information about any business topic, including personal brands. I've read multiple articles in both *HBR* and other business literature that look at personal brand within the context of a corporate organization. How can you build your personal brand to make yourself more promotable? The term *intentional* is often used to describe the process of building a personal brand. One has to intentionally build their brand, so it seems.

You do have to be intentional about your personal brand because it's what you say *and* what you do that builds your brand. In this case, doing speaks more loudly than saying. If you want to have a personal brand of providing great service, but you don't' provide great service, then that isn't your personal brand no matter how much you wish it to be so. Action is the biggest component of intentionality. If you don't act in a fashion that is congruent with your brand, then, no matter your intentions, it isn't your personal brand.

Personalbrands.com, which brands itself as the "leading authority on the topic of personal branding," will tell you that most of the personal brand definitions out there on the internet aren't very good. They say something to the effect that a personal brand is the uniform perception or impression of an individual based on experience, expertise, and so forth. They also note that personal branding (as opposed to personal brand) is the effort that goes into communicating your personal brand to the world. I can agree with that last statement.

Sidebar, please, Your Honor. I'd like to talk about three things that I find troubling in the Personalbrands.com statement. The first is their use of superlatives—"the leading authority." We'll have more to say about superlatives later in the book, but let's briefly explore this particular "leading authority" claim. It is possible that they are the leading authority, but wouldn't it be better for someone else to call you this than for you to proclaim this for yourself? When this is a self-proclaimed honor, it also implicitly carries some baggage, such as bragging, which most people find unattractive.

Since we're talking about bragging, the second issue that I have with this statement is the lack of humility. Any self-proclamation of greatness, outside of Muhammed Ali calling himself "the greatest" (because he actually was the greatest heavyweight boxer of his generation), is not humble. It says to me that someone or some organization is doing its own grading, and I don't think that's right. It's far better, in my opinion, to say that you strive for greatness or that you strive to provide excellent products or services to your clients. Ultimately, the client is the judge of greatness and excellence. Any superlative self-proclamations with respect to personal brand really just come across as arrogance, not greatness.

Finally, there is a self-awareness component to a personal brand that seems to be overpowered by the self-proclaimed greatness. Arrogance or extreme self-confidence are usually not good components of a personal brand. I would say that measured self-confidence shows a high level of emotional intelligence and self-awareness as compared with using superlatives. Again, I'll refer to Muhammed Ali. He called himself "the greatest" in a sport where self-promotion must be backed up by performance. In his case, it most certainly was. Normally, I'm not a fan of braggadocio or cockiness. For Muhammad Ali, it was simply fact; he was the greatest, and he had the track record to back that up. Has your personal brand beaten all the top contenders in the boxing ring? If not, you might want to swallow a dose of humble self-awareness and be much more realistic about how you present yourself.

Experience as a Brand Differentiator

At some point in time, we need to discuss why client experience is such a powerful brand differentiator. Now is that time, before we get to *brand convergence*.

Let's start with why people make purchase decisions. You know from your own experience that there exists a very wide spectrum by which you make a purchasing decision. It could be cost (high or low), quality, convenience, peer pressure, ability to return if you don't like it, it was there adjacent to the checkout line, or your mom asked you to buy that specific brand. There are many, many more.

Good marketers know that they need to tune their marketing to the point in the "purchase decision spectrum" that consumers most closely align with their product or service. Sur Coffee in Orange County does this. They have a surfer vibe that permeates their business. They sell coffee that they purchase from small farmers in South America, use a proprietary roasting process, have really friendly and kind staff, and serve a reasonably priced, really delicious cup of coffee (along with some outstanding pastries). What's the purchase decision for a coffee place like Sur? Convenience is one; it's in a good location, pretty close to some of the best surf spots. Community is another; the surfers like to hang out at Sur, and Sur makes it easy for them to do so. Quality is another; I'll drive an extra five miles to get coffee at Sur because it's simply better. They've put together a system that works with how their target market makes purchasing decisions. The total experience becomes the differentiator.

One more thought on this topic revolves around quality and value. It is very hard for most people to fully understand comparative product or service quality or value. We all try, but it's just hard. I recently purchased some T-shirts through an online company that offered a very unique experience. They sent me three shirts to try on (after I gave them some basic sizing information) along with three swatches of fabric. I tried the shirts, picked the one that fit me the best, and sent the other two shirts back to them.

Based on the trial, I decided to order some additional shirts. The interesting thing had to do with the three types of fabric that they offered. It was very hard for me to tell the difference, so I went to their website, which had a "fabric tutorial." This was OK, but without seeing the actual shirts, it's really hard to tell what they'll look like from a tutorial that talks about thread count and a swatch that's two inches by two inches in size. Additionally, each fabric type is a different price point. Who knows which would be the best value for me. I just bought the most expensive ones, using price as my quality differentiator. Using the fabric swatch, I just couldn't tell which one was better.

The shirts arrived, and the fabric differed from my expectations. I then decided to purchase a couple of their shirts with the most popular fabric option that also happens to have the lowest price point in their family of products. As it turned out, I preferred this fabric, but there was no technical reason; I just liked it better.

It is very hard for people to ascertain value and quality. Do you know how a Ford F-150 compares to a Dodge Ram, Nissan Armada, Toyota Tacoma, or Chevrolet Silverado? You likely have a preference, and you may actually have a rational reason for choosing one over another. Or you may be influenced by family, friends, advertising, pricing, proximity of the dealer, or your experience with the dealer. When you don't know which is really the best value or the best quality, you devolve to experience.

The intersection of customer value and purchasing decisions is depicted graphically in figure 1. I'm using a Harvard Business

School–inspired two-by-two matrix as a way of showing how client experience can create a strong brand.

The x-axis shows the purchase decision spectrum. This ranges from price and/or convenience on the left to client experience on the right. The y-axis is the client-perceived value of the product or service, ranging from low to high. Low might be a bag of potato chips, and on the high end are things like cars, professional services (medical, dental, legal, etc.), and luxury goods—big-ticket items.

The bottom left quadrant is where consumers make a purchase decision based on price or convenience, usually for services or products that they consider to be undifferentiated with respect to quality. In fact, in this quadrant, branding probably doesn't matter all that much. You drive to the closest market to pick up a loaf of bread. You go to the nail salon that you can easily get to by walking. Those are convenience decisions. You go to the gas station with the lowest prices. You choose to get your hair cut at the local beauty school (I think this might be risky decision, but I've never done it, so I don't know for sure). These are cost decisions. That's it; cost and maybe convenience, to a limited extent, are all that matter.

The upper left quadrant is where value matters to the purchaser. Their decision to buy their new espresso machine relies upon reviews and a perception of value; a consumer may put three or four similar machines in the "best value" box and then make a price-based decision. They may do some research on both the product or service and the establishment from which they procure the product or service. This will be the best that they can do. It's very hard to tell the difference, but they'll do some math to satisfy themselves that they bought the best.

This is often how cars are purchased. A consumer will try to find the perfect car that fits into their suite of criteria, such as size, fuel efficiency, reliability, color, sunroof, stereo system, and many others. Once they narrow down their search to their top two or three options, they will find one criterion that is most important them and then make their purchase decision. Best value and best quality will get them to a short list of options and may even be the criteria upon which they make a decision. Those terms—value and quality—will mean something different to every car buyer. Thus, it is hard for the car companies to promote their products based on value and quality because these are fuzzy concepts in the minds of most consumers.

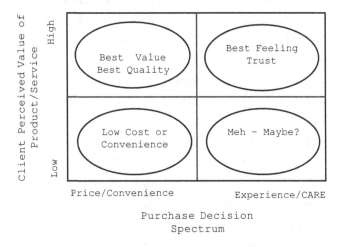

Figure 1. The value of experience as a brand differentiator

The lower right quadrant is where consumers make a purchase decision based on their experience with the product, service, or retail establishment. A consumer might go an extra mile to purchase the six-pack of beer at the retail store where they know that they'll get a polite greeting and some assistance from the employees in making their selection of a product from a local craft brewery. What if that employee is not working at that time? They got great assistance the last time they came in to buy something, but this time no one seems able to help them. The consumer is lost. Should they come back another day? Should they make a purchase even though they aren't sure that they are doing the right thing? Should they go back to the closer store and try them? This is a tough one, and the answer to all of their questions is the very unsatisfying "I don't know." This is a big *meh* for the consumer.

They like the experience component of the transaction, but they don't always get it, and they don't know if the extra drive (or walk, or bike ride) is worth it.

The upper right quadrant is where high customer-perceived value meets great experience. The ability to consistently deliver great experience results in the development of a raving fan, a customer who will come back time after time to purchase products or services from your company. This is often the case for expensive or luxury goods or services, but it is not limited to these categories.

Pacific Sales is one such company that lives in this upper right quadrant. This company sells nice kitchen, bath, and outdoor BBQ appliances. I've used them several times and always felt that the salesperson gave me good advice on the products I was purchasing. They delivered the products on time, and every product has worked fantastically with no issues.

What was the experience? They were honest brokers. They could have steered us to more expensive appliances, but they understood what we wanted and helped us without upselling us into something we didn't need. In some cases, we did buy the more expensive appliance because we felt it best met our needs. The bottom line is that we needed technical guidance, and we found an organization that provides honest technical input.

Experience is powerful because it is so memorable. Think about a great concert that you saw or a fabulous trip that you took. Think about getting stuck in an airport due to a storm or a problem with your plane or getting bad news about the cost of a repair for your car. Experiences stick in our minds—both positive and negative. It's not always the big things. More often, as David Maister says, it's a thousand little things that add up to a good or bad experience. Would you like some examples? Sure, I've got some.

Here's a negative example. I came into possession of a 1920s vintage Waterman Ideal leak-proof fountain pen. This pen, which belonged to my father, has a bladder that holds the ink and a small lever that pops out of the side of the pen to pump the ink into the bladder. Knowing that the pen had not been used in decades, I decided to have it checked over by an expert rather than filling it with ink to test its leak-proof-ness.

There aren't many fountain pen repair experts around, but I found one near my office in Pasadena, California. This shop was located in an industrial strip mall, and upon entering, I knew I was in the right place because there were hundreds of fountain pens in display cases and the person behind the counter looked old enough that he might have personally known Mr. Waterman.

The person behind the counter was the owner, and he asked me what I wanted. I showed him my pen and asked what he would recommend. He told me that he would replace the bladder and make sure that the pump/lever worked. He had a flat price of one hundred dollars, and he told me that it would be at least three weeks before he could get it done because he was "very busy" and had to go to a "pen convention" in two weeks' time (and he had to prepare for that). He was very abrupt with me and told me to quickly decide because he was—not to put too fine a point on it—very busy. I was the only customer in the shop. But he was busy.

Three weeks came and went. I waited five weeks and called to find out the status of my pen. One of the owner's employees answered the phone. I told her my name and described my pen and asked if perhaps the repairs had been completed. This person asked me when I had dropped the pen off for repairs. I replied that it was five weeks ago. "Hah!" the employee screamed at me. "He's very busy, and we can't be bothered with your calls. We'll call you when it's done." Fair enough. When you are the only game in town, you get to make the rules.

I did finally get the pen, and it worked beautifully. It only took eight weeks, and for the record, I had to call them to find out if it was ready. Apparently, no one in that shop knew how to make an outgoing call on a touch tone phone. Often, it only takes one crazy thing to make a memorable bad experience.

Apple provides a positive experience. I cannot think of any time that I was in an Apple store where I was not pleasantly surprised. I wanted to buy an iPad for one of my sons, who, at that time, lived in Manhattan. We went to the Chelsea Apple store, and they told us that this particular iPad was a very popular product and that they had none in stock. They checked at the Soho Apple store, which had three left. I asked if they could reserve one for us, which they did, and my son got his graduation gift!

Apple does the little things right. They patiently provide information. I'll stop in to ask about the best way to use an app, and someone will always help me. They let me sit at a big table and transfer stuff to my new iPhone even though I could have easily done this at home. I just wasn't absolutely sure that I knew what I was doing, so they indulged me (and many others as well). The consistent positive experience is what differentiates Apple. Is this available from other technology manufacturers that have their own retail stores? It probably is, but for me, I *trust* that I will have a great *experience* at an Apple retail store—and I'm sticking with them because of that trust and experience.

Client experience matters. Who creates that experience? Your employees do this. Let's look at how this works.

Brand Convergence

At the heart of all of this is the idea of brand convergence. Simply put, this is the synergistic merging of personal and corporate brands in the eyes of the client. Your corporate brand is so perfectly supported by the personal brand of the individual, or individuals, working with your client that there is a synergy that positively and lastingly differentiates your company from your competitors.

"Why" Is the Key

Another way to look at this is that brand convergence happens when the company's *why* is congruent with the employee's *why*. That is, the reason the company is doing something like trying to provide great service is that they want to take care of their clients in a way that no other company in their industry is doing. If the employees who are client facing want to do the same thing, you have brand convergence.

This is so important that I want to devote some thoughts to this topic for all of us who are employees working in the business world and trying to do a great job.

Our lives are full of things that we do. We have a job, family, friends, volunteer gigs, hobbies, and avocations. We go to work for forty hours each week (or more) and engage in activities with our coworkers, customers, clients, and business partners. Work activities make up a big chunk of our lives; work provides the funding for everything else that we do with family and friends. It's a massive time commitment, and once you sort out why in the context of your life and your job, it can make things easier and better. You, as an individual, need to figure out your *why* and how it meshes with your company's *why*.

What Is "Why"?

Why is less about what you do and more about what you give, or want to give, to society. Winston Churchill said, "We make a living by what we give." That seems like a good starting point for our *why* in the context of work. Yes, we need to make a living so we can take care of ourselves and our families, but we also can adapt our approach to our work so that it encompasses giving. The term *giving* can refer to lots of things. It does not solely refer to money or time.

Researchers give us cures and vaccines; business leaders give us opportunities to succeed and improve; authors give us opportunities to learn; engineers give us buildings, cars, highways, clean water, and lots more; teachers give us knowledge; advisors give us wisdom. The list can go on and on. Everyone on this list earns money through their work. They also earn deep self-satisfaction and joy through what they give. It is a shift in focus away from money; it is a focus on your understanding of why you do what you do. You focus less on what you get and more on what you give—and when you do, you find that your work is much more satisfying.

Your *why* can evolve over time, and it may be different as you change companies or move up the career ladder. This certainly was the case for me. When I first started working, I wanted to help bring clean water to the world. The demands of work, family, and career goals moved me away from helping people to wanting to focus on my own career.

Over time, I realized through a series of circumstances that the things that gave me the most satisfaction were working with our clients to help them solve their complex problems and working with our staff to help them build their careers. That ultimately became my *why*. It only took me three decades to really find it and weave it into my daily work. I'm fortunate that I work in the engineering consulting world, where client service is an important aspect of what we do. I also have a lecturer position at a great university, where I can pour out my experience for students and I can use decades of industry connections to help them as they seek out internships and information on industries that are of interest to them.

How to Find "Why"

Why is about what you give, in the context of your job, that results in great satisfaction and joy for you. There is no formula. There is no guidebook or instruction manual. There is only you. What gives you the greatest satisfaction? What gives you joy? What makes you feel fulfilled? This isn't about your hobbies or avocations. This is not about making money. Everyone wants to earn enough money to support themselves and their families. Earning money is a basic need, not a *why*.

Avocations and hobbies are great. I hope you have these in your life. You may experience great joy when you play music for others or play in your weekly softball league. You may get great satisfaction from producing a piece of artwork or penning the next great mystery novel. Very few people can make a living through their hobbies or avocations. If you can make your living in sports, art, music, or literature, then you may have found your *why*, but very few people are professional athletes, musicians, artists, or authors. Most of us need our jobs to earn our livings, and we need to find out our *why* in the context of our jobs.

What gives you joy or great satisfaction in your job? This is something that may take time or even a bit of introspection (I know introspection can be scary for a lot of people). It also may be something that you can sort out by simply changing your frame of reference—by honestly trying to answer what, in your job, gives you the greatest satisfaction. It does not matter what you do for a living. You might derive the greatest joy from being pleasant and friendly to people. Or you might get great satisfaction from simply doing your job very well. Does that make a difference? Does that change the world? It very well might. You never know how you can positively impact someone from a kind word, a pleasant interaction, or a job done well. If that gives you joy, then that may be your *why*.

In the end, your understanding of *why* is a win-win. You'll make the lives of others better, and you'll derive greater satisfaction and joy from what you do. When your *why* converges with your company's *why*, then you've won the trifecta of business—everything is better. It doesn't have to just be business.

One of my sons had a job as a religious studies professor in a community college system. He was constantly trying to get his students to think differently about a variety of topics. He gets great joy when he gets feedback from a student who tells him that the course has really changed their perspective. That is his *why*. I've heard it directly from his students. One morning, my son was visiting us and had an early-morning class that he was teaching online. After the class, he had a discussion with one of his students that I overheard. The student told him multiple times what a great job he was doing, to keep it up, and "what classes are you teaching next semester so I can sign up for one of them." Isn't that what education is all about—getting people to be passionate about learning? Yes, I think it is, and I think that's a great example of brand convergence.

We all know lawyers who really strive to help people, nurses who get job satisfaction from being kind to people in need, volunteers who love a personal interaction that lifts someone's spirits, scientists and engineers who derive satisfaction from contributing to the body of knowledge in their chosen field, and that person in the local coffee shop who has the ability to brighten your day with a smile and kind word.

Your *why* can certainly change over time. I suspect that it does for the vast majority of people. When you focus on *why* you are doing something, when you focus on how your work enables you to give to others, then you will understand the value and satisfaction one can get from their job. You'll know your *why*.

The Spectrum of Brand Convergence

Brand convergence isn't a point in time or a point on a graph. It's so much more nuanced than that. Figure 2 shows my version of a brand convergence matrix.

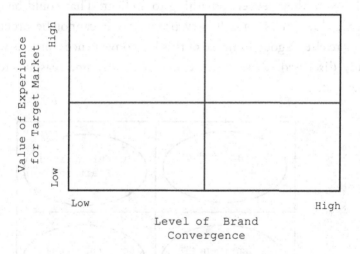

Figure 2. Brand convergence matrix

This is a simple way of looking at this concept. The level of brand convergence that exists within your organization is on the x-axis ranging from low to high. Along the y-axis is the level at which your target market values *experience*. This is the experience that your clients have in dealing with your company.

This matters because, if you want to make a better experience part of your brand, you have to consider how that experience will be delivered, and it will almost always be delivered through a person who works for your company and interacts with a client.

Figure 3 shows what brand convergence can mean for your company and your company's brand.

There are multiple potential outcomes; for simplicity, we'll look at four. Let's start in the lower left quadrant. Here, your target market doesn't value a brand differentiated on experience. They won't normally care what your employees are like. They have something that they want to buy, and they are making their purchase based on something other than experience or trust—normally something like price or convenience.

In this case, brand convergence doesn't matter. Experience doesn't matter. Your employees don't have to represent your brand other than making sure they deliver something to a client. That could be convenience, low prices, or a luxury product that cannot be procured anywhere else. A good example of this is a convenience store. As we've already discussed, these stores exist for mostly one reason—to be convenient.

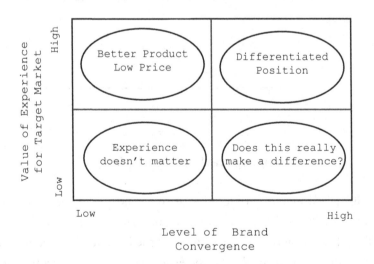

Figure 3. Brand convergence outcomes

Companies in the lower right quadrant have high brand convergence but a target market that doesn't care about having a great experience. Imagine you run a car wash where everyone is friendly and works hard to get every last water spot off your car. You have a competitive price and a great service. Your customers in this case will focus on the product or service, and your brand will be about the outcome rather than the process. Your employees can be grumpy misanthropes; it won't matter as long as the car is spotless *and* the price doesn't go up. The question that this book attempts to answer is, is this really true? Could experience make a difference with this target market? Could a portion of this market respond to a company positioned around client experience?

Another example of this is fast fashion retailers. Many of the sales associates working in a fast fashion retail store are also true believers in the products that their stores offer. There is high brand convergence. Do the people who are purchasing fast fashion care about the experience? Are they looking for a great experience, or are they just looking for low prices on trendy clothes? Could experience be a differentiator for a fast fashion retailer? I think it can.

Some companies have target markets that do care about experience. Companies that exist in the upper left quadrant strive to offer a great client experience but struggle to do so because their people are not committed to delivering this experience. This is brand divergence. Consider an accountancy practice that focuses on tax returns. The accountants are competent and efficient. The firm completes your tax return in a timely manner. It is emailed to you by their receptionist with no cover letter; it simply says, "Here's your tax return." You see something that you think is an error, and you respond with an email identifying this error and saying that you hope that they haven't submitted this to the IRS and state government. The receptionist sends you a scathing email in return, saying that you are foolish for thinking that they would do this without your approval and a few other choice things about your competence as a human being. That firm isn't providing a great experience, so they had better offer a better product or a better price, or you'll move on. This is also brand divergence, and this happened to me just once. I found another mechanism to complete my taxes without fear of the raging receptionist.

The really bad experiences that I've had with the service departments of luxury car dealers is another example of an organization that fits into this quadrant. It's a luxury car, so I expect excellence, a high level of communication, and attention to details. The people working there were very nice but completely nonresponsive to me. Experience matters for high-end products and the services associated with them. Sure, they offered me a cup of coffee and a nice pastry, but what I really wanted was my car fixed right and fixed on time. Those things, I didn't get them. Brand divergence.

Brand divergence will cost you clients. They'll go somewhere that gives them a great experience while still delivering high-quality service and products.

The upper right quadrant is the goal. Here, your target market highly values the experience they have in dealing with your company, and everyone in your company delivers. You have a differentiated position. You have a clientele that is unlikely to leave you as long as you continue to deliver a great experience for them.

Tiffany's is a great example of this. I'm not a big Tiffany's shopper, so I only get the experience that they offer to the unwashed masses. It's very good. I've always felt good about myself and my purchase, notwithstanding the fact that I spent a lot more money than I had intended to spend at the point in time when I walked into the store. For those who are regulars at Tiffany's in New York City, there are special floors in their building that can only be accessed by their most loyal clientele, providing the best shopping experience for these clients, with Tiffany's employees who are trained to make it a great experience. That's real brand convergence.

This whole concept is easy to mess up. Often, it takes only one or two people to not exhibit the right personal brand, and your overall corporate brand is blown up. Think about the following in a business context. Your company wants to, for example, be known for extraordinary service to your clients. What happens if one of your employees is actually rude to a client?

Many years ago, a church (I know that a church is not a company, but it is an organization that has a brand, with people who have personal brands) in Southern California decided to have a bumper sticker campaign. That's right—bumper stickers. These are the nominally ten-inch by three-inch, rectangular pieces of PVC stuck to the bumper of a personal vehicle, with pithy sayings such as "Baby on Board," "Keep on Truckin'," "My other car is a Tardis," or my personal favorite, "Jesus would have let me merge in."

The leadership of this church determined that a great way to get people to come to their church was to pass out bumper stickers to their members that said "XYZ Church, the Friendly Ones." This was capped off by a happy face, and, of course, the bumper sticker was yellow with black lettering and graphics.

OK, a local church decided to do a little promotion using bumper stickers; is that really so bad? Churches do stuff all the time. Churches put ads on social media or in local papers to advise people of the schedule for their Easter or Christmas services. Churches promote their music, or their service times, or their food banks, or their social events for senior citizens (I mistakenly got one of these emails). There's nothing wrong with any of these things.

The bumper sticker, on the other hand, was probably a massive mistake. Here are just two reasons why I think this bumper sticker campaign, in particular, is in the Marketing Hall of Fame for dumb ideas.

First, it's arrogant and insulting. You may consider those to be separate reasons, but for brevity, I'm lumping them into one. Who says that you are the "friendly ones"? What makes you friendlier than other churches that pretty much share the same core beliefs with you? What does *friendly* even mean in this context? It's arrogant to think that you are better than others. It's insulting to those who attend other churches and are also friendly people, and I'm not sure that it is the best exemplar of the teachings of Jesus. That's just the first reason.

The second may be more relatable to the business world. What if, and I'm just guessing here, one person who visited that church on any given Sunday interacted with any church member who was unfriendly or unhelpful. It's hard to imagine that such a scenario could be possible, but just work with me on this. Such unfriendliness or unhelpfulness is defined by the visitor, not the church member. The church member might think that they are offering helpful advice on the appropriate attire to wear to church, where the visitor should park, what the pastor of the church is like, and other externalities related to church attendance. What if that unfriendliness or unhelpfulness toward the visitor manifested itself in a manner akin to Dana Carvey's "Church Lady" character from the *Saturday Night Live* shows of yore? Today, it only takes one person to post stuff on social media after a bad interaction with the "Church Lady." If that happens, then your premise of being the "friendly ones" goes right out the stained glass window. "Now isn't that special?"

The third reason has to do with the car on which the bumper sticker resides. Again, this is just a hypothetical, but what if the driver with said "friendly ones" bumper sticker is a lousy driver, mean driver, horn honker, or any other type of driver that can irritate others who are on the road? Would you be persuaded by the bumper sticker? Or would you be dissuaded by the driver's behavior?

Your employees need to be invested in your brand. Their personal brand needs to be convergent with your company's brand.

Maybe that's all that needs to be said about this topic, and you can now close this book up, switch your phone to some music, or go watch a rerun of your favorite crime show on your favorite streaming service. I'm totally fine if you want to do that. Or you can read on for a bit more, and we can dig more into the concept of personal brand and brand convergence. Why should you do that? It just might help you figure out how you can use the concept of CARE in your branding and get both your corporate brand and the personal brand of your client-facing staff synchronized.

CHAPTER TWO

CARE for Your Clients

Abetter experience can be part of the brand that you build to set your company apart from your competition. We've already discussed how such a brand requires your client-facing employees to adapt and accept this as their personal brand. What exactly are you asking them to do? You have to ask them to do something. Simply telling all staff to be "friendly," or that the "client is always right" is not sufficient to build a sustainable and sufficiently differentiated brand.

Over forty years in engineering and construction, I've been involved in some of our company's biggest marketing campaigns, and I've asked dozens of clients how they have made purchasing decisions. I also know a little bit about how individuals buy professional services to meet their own needs. In just about every major purchase decision, the two over-riding factors are "best feeling" and "trust."

That's for big stuff. What about for other things that we buy? Can "best feeling" and "trust" factor into these purchase decisions? I think they can. Sometimes we need an energy drink at 7:00 a.m. from a convenience store conveniently located in San Clemente; this is a convenience decision. Other times, we have options, and when you have options, many other factors can be part of your decision-making process.

Consistently providing a great experience requires some general guidelines that drive employees' mental models with respect to client interactions. I developed a simple and (I think) memorable set of guide-lines that fits into the acronym CARE. This is a set of general principles that employees can use to establish a baseline for client experience. Here's a quick summary:

> C—communication. This is about face-to-face and electronic communication with a client. How do you communicate with a client or potential client? How do you provide information to them? How do you speak with them? Communication is one of the ways clients form opinions of your products or services.

> A—attention. This is about listening to and showing respect to a client. How well do you listen and under-stand a client's needs? How do you show them respect? How do you make them feel important?

> R—responsiveness. This is doing what you said you would do, when you said you would do it. It's also about answering the phone. Are you on time? Do you value your client's time? Do you respond promptly to texts or emails? Do you answer your phone when the client calls?

> E—excellence. This is about providing excellence, as your client defines it, to your clients. Do you know how your client would define excellence in the products or services that your company provides to them?

There is a lot more to be said about each of these. We'll address them one by one with lots of examples.

C–Communication

Communication is the art of conveying and receiving information. This is what you do with clients. You interact with them through some mode of communication. It could be verbal, nonverbal (like a nod or a smile), electronic, or nothing (that's also called ignoring people). If you communicate well, you'll enhance your client relationships and begin to build trust with that client.

Every person on this planet has preferences for how they like to communicate with others and how they like others to communicate with them. Those preferences are, at a minimum, situational and temporal; they depend on the specific situation and the time within that situation. There are undoubtedly other factors involved, on top of these. This is what makes great communication with your client so difficult.

In the marketing world, promotion and pricing are two significant means of communicating information with clients. We aren't going to talk about these aspects of communication. We're going to focus on interpersonal communication—person to person, the hardest kind of communication to do well. It's also one of the most significant ways you can convey your company's brand to your client.

Are you appreciative when a service provider communicates with you? Do you recall an instance where your doctor, dentist, nail salon person, or some other service provider took the time to talk with you about details? Perhaps you appreciated a clerk in a department store telling you, "I'll be with you in two minutes." Maybe your electrician called you to make sure the new fan they installed is working well, giving you an opportunity to have them come back to your house because it wasn't working well. Communication is a big part of service and a fantastic mechanism for creating great client experience.

Communication is about two-way communication with your client. It could be verbal, phone conversations, or face-to-face interactions. It could be written—text messages, emails, or letters. It can be nonverbal—a nod, a smile, or a wave (or sometimes it can devolve into a select part of the hand). It can be third party—the main service provider sends an intermediary to deliver a message or collect information necessary to the completion of the transaction. It can be a noise—a cough, a grunt, a laugh.

Communication may start with client preferences. In many situations, you will have a client who will indicate (through some type of communication with you) their preferred method of communication. Another aspect of communication is simply, what are you communicating? Finally, the least appreciated element of communication is explanations and excuses.

Let's explore multiple aspects of client communications. We'll stay away from inappropriate communications because you have likely had some corporate training on things that you shouldn't say or do (commonly known as inappropriate behavior). If you haven't suffered through these training videos, you, as a human being, know there are things that are inappropriate and that shouldn't be said or done when dealing with clients. Let's leave it at that and focus on the positive ways of understanding client communications.

Why Do We Communicate with Each Other?

This is the basic framework for communications between an individual who represents a business and a client, or potential client. Why do we, in a commercial transaction, communicate with each other? Let's start with this and then move on to some more practical realities of communication.

1. *Establish a relationship.* The first step in communication is establishing a relationship with the client. This is obviously not a BFF-type relationship. Rather, it's a business relationship that may last for a few seconds or for years. You are not trying to turn this client into a close friend who gets invited to family parties. You are simply trying to do the most basic aspects of establishing contact with another individual, and that starts with

a greeting and recognition of their existence. You might even tell them your name if you are so inclined. I happen to think this is a good inclination in most business transactions. It's the start and nothing more.

2. *Understand client needs.* Sometimes a person browsing through the shoe section of a department store is doing nothing more than killing time. Their need may be that they want to be left alone and allowed to kill time in a humane and professional manner. (Many of us are professional time killers. I prefer the news feed on my phone as my primary mode, but if there is no place to sit, I'll gladly browse through the shoe section as my first alternate choice.) Their need may be that they are actually looking for shoes and are potential shoe buyers. They will let you know if they are asked.

3. *Convey information.* As the representative of a business, you may have information about a product or service that would be of use to a client. Your role is to provide this information if you are asked to provide it. We'll discuss this in more detail a bit further along in this section.

4. *Make the deal.* In retail settings, communication is required to close a deal. Even my convenience store friend had to communicate with me by head nods and hand motions to complete my energy drink purchase transaction. Professional service providers also communicate to establish a scope of work and agree upon a price and schedule for the service.

Communication Preferences

Great service providers know how to communicate with their clients on the terms that are most suitable for the client. This simply means that you do this in a way that works best for your client.

I had a big construction project in Utah. I was living in Denver and was committed to being at the project one day a month. That was not enough. Frequent communication is an absolute necessity on big construction projects; you want to talk with the client about accomplishments the previous week, plans for the next two weeks, any issues you are facing, and what you are trying to do to overcome those issues. I tried calling my client weekly, but he was not a big phone talker. We just didn't connect well over the phone; it wasn't his problem (it might have been me; who knows?), but it wasn't working well.

The on-site project manager was a guy named Ben. I deputized him to have this "last week, next two weeks, problems/actions" conversation with the client. My client came to work at 6:00 a.m. on Monday morning, so I asked Ben to go over to his office, bring some doughnuts, and have this fifteen-minute conversation. Then ask the client if this is a good way to communicate this information to him—if he is comfortable with this approach. It worked beautifully. Ben appreciated the time to interact with the client, and the client appreciated the opportunity to interact with Ben. It was communication on the client's terms.

Well, that's great for $100 million construction projects. What about interactions in other retail or service settings? Preferences are just as important. How do you greet someone when they walk into your store? How do you indicate willingness to be available to a potential client in a store? What are you communicating to them?

Businesses handle this "How to communicate?" question very differently. Some have employees enthusiastically scream, "Welcome into XXXX Subs and Sandwiches!" Some merely nod or smile at customers. Some ask, "Is there anything I can do to help you?" You may make this initial interaction part of your brand, or you may leave it up to your employees. Here are a few things to consider:

1. Not everyone needs help, but people do like to be acknowledged. In some way, you should acknowledge people. A smile, a polite nod, a warm "Good afternoon," or "Please let me know if I can help you" are among the ways to do this.
2. Don't force yourself on people. Not everyone wants or needs your help.

3. Make yourself available. Don't disappear into the back room. Don't hide behind a counter yapping with your coworker.
4. Don't stalk a client. Give them space. Be respectfully available.
5. You can read body language, especially a confused look on someone's face. It's OK to ask a second time if they need assistance. Three times is definitely too much.

I was asked to get some kind of vaping device for a family member who was ill and didn't feel that they could get it themselves. Just to demonstrate my utter ignorance of this product, I told the family member that I would go to Target to procure the device (the name and description of which they had written down on paper for my benefit). "Oh no," I was told. "Target doesn't carry this device. You have to go to (the name of a convenience store different from the one I referred to earlier in the book)."

Off I went, and to my surprise, all of these devices were behind a counter, and there appeared to be dozens of options—maybe more. Nothing exactly matched what was on my little cheat sheet of vaping devices. I was just staring at the wall of vaping stuff. The clerk concluded a transaction, looked at me, and very kindly asked if she could help me out. I showed her my note, saying that I knew nothing about these products. She said, "Oh, I know exactly what you need. Here it is, and it's two fourteen." My response was immediate—faster than a top-end electric vehicle in a 0 to 60 mph test, I responded, "Are you kidding? Two hundred and fourteen dollars?" Acknowledging my ignorance with a smirk, she said, "Nope. Two dollars and fourteen cents."

She simply asked. That's the first step in communication. Do you have a need? Sometimes the client wants help, and sometimes the client says no. In my particular case, I said yes, even though I found it a bit embarrassing that I knew nothing about vaping. When someone says no, just be respectfully available in case they get over their embarrassment.

Clients will tell you their communication preferences if you listen, have rudimentary body-language reading skills, and pay attention to what they are doing and how they are acting.

What to Communicate

Businesses have a lot of things to say to their clients. You may wish to tell your client how you are better than the competition, how you best fit their needs, how you can save them time and money, how you are "just looking out for them," and more. Business communications can be categorized in a number of ways. We're going to explore the following specific things to communicate to your client: setting expectations, filling in the narrative, delivering news, managing bad news, explanations, and excuses.

Setting Expectations

Every client who engages your business has a set of expectations. Your business may, or may not, be able to meet those expectations. You likely have a very good idea of the most significant elements of your clients' expectations. If you own a tire shop, someone coming into your shop needs new tires, or needs some pricing information, or perhaps some timing information (how quickly could you get these odd-sized tires). Someone walking into a tax preparation business before April 15 needs their tax returns prepared. If they are coming into your tax preparation business after April 15, they likely have some additional issues associated with their need to have their tax returns prepared.

It's not always that easy. Someone wandering around the shoe department of a Macy's may be browsing, killing time, or looking for something specific. Those are widely varying sets of expectations, and you can only find out by asking.

Service providers and retailers often have to set expectations for their customers. Those expectations are generally around quality, schedule, and cost. At a shoe store, I asked if they had a particular shoe in my size. They didn't, but they offered to call around and find it for me at another store. I accepted their offer, and they informed me that their Las Vegas store had the shoes in my size and could ship those to me at no additional cost. "Great. When can I get them?" "Two weeks, maybe three weeks," was the answer. They set expectations that, in this instance, didn't meet my needs, and I didn't get the shoes. If they hadn't, I might have purchased the shoes and then been upset at the long delivery time.

Service providers often need to set expectations around what they can and cannot do. In some cases, they set expectations around what can go wrong. I was required to visit an endodontist to fix an issue with a tooth. He started out his service by explaining what he was going to do, how long it would take, what I could expect, when I was going feel pain, when I would be blissfully numb, and, finally, what might go wrong. It wasn't the "what" that I found interesting. It was the way the endodontist explained it. They started with an apology. "I apologize, but it's possible that the tip of the drill bit might break off in the root of your tooth. It won't affect anything. You'll simply have some metallic rein-forcement in there. Just letting you know, and I'm sorry if it happens." It all seemed pretty logical to me, and I'm pretty sure I've got a drill bit floating around in the root of one of my molars.

Let your customers know what you can do and let them know what you can't do.

Filling in the Narrative

Business interactions often take place over a period of time. In some cases, there are multiple interactions between the business and the cus-tomer until the transaction is complete. That transaction has a narrative.

Let's break that down, starting with the term *narrative*. Using my trusty *Merriam-Webster Dictionary* app, narrative means, among other things, "a way of presenting or understanding a situation or series of events that reflects and promotes a particular point of view."

An author named Brené Brown wrote, "In the absence of data, we will always make up stories." With respect to this chapter of the book, "data" is "communication." I like to rephrase Brené Brown's quote like this: "In the absence of a narrative, the client makes up their own story, and it's usually negative."

There is a point of view involved in this, and it belongs to your client, not to your business. In any transaction, the client is thinking about themselves—and pretty much only themselves. Of course, there are clients in restaurants who are thinking about leaving a nice tip for the waitstaff as a reward for great service, or clients buying products that support society (e.g., buy one, and we give one to underserved communities) or the environment (e.g., buy our sustainably made product). Other than that, most transactions are about the client. Are they getting what they want? Is it working out for them? Are they happy, and will they rave about your store or professional services firm to their friends?

Narratives have a time element, so punctuality may be part of the narrative. Were you ready for me when I showed up on time for my 10:00 a.m. appointment, or did you make me wait? How long do I need to wait in the return line, and why is that employee walking away from the sales point, so now it looks like my wait is going to be much longer? Can you describe the comparative quality of two different products that appear to be the same price?

Narratives may have a quality element. "The last time we ate here, the food was great, and this time it's mediocre. Why?" "I spent a lot of money on this car, and it seems to have some ongoing problems." "Wouldn't it be nice if the Wi-Fi worked on this flight so I could watch a movie?"

Narratives have a cost element. This happens every time you buy a new car. The list price is $30,000, and then there are taxes, license fees, destination charges, and suddenly you are at $34,000. Now you have to run the gauntlet of extras and upsell that the car dealer *drives* you through. And I mean *drive* as in driving cattle. You had an expectation of paying $30,000, and now you are paying 20 percent more; there's a negative narrative here.

Narratives are often wrapped around a client's needs and expectations. When those aren't met, the client has a story—a narrative that

CARE for Your Clients

tells them whether they are happy or sad with their interaction with your business.

Not every business interaction has a narrative. Honestly, I didn't need advice from the convenience store guy. I just needed him to ring up my purchase so I could pay and be on my way. That's not always true. You don't know who has needs and who doesn't. You have to ask. You might get shot down with a dagger-like stare that says, "Don't talk to me." That's great; you have your answer. You asked, and they told you unequivocally what they wanted.

A client's point of view is going to be different for varying retail and service transactions. When the dentist is telling me that I need some complex thing done to my mouth, I want them to explain a couple of things: how long it will take, what it will cost, and how they will keep me pain-free throughout. Dentists know this and are very good about it. The same is true of most health care providers, with, in my opinion, one exception. That exception is when they bring out any type of needle and say, "This will only hurt a little bit ... just a tiny prick." Maybe I don't understand the concept of a "tiny prick," but it always seems to hurt more than that. Sorry to digress.

Outside of the pain part, timing, cost, and quality are the big three elements for professional service provider communication. When can I get this done, and how long will it take? What is it going to cost? What's the quality? How long will it last? Is this the best I can get? And so on. Any service provider should be able to tell you these things. Let's look at a couple of examples.

We have a plumber named Marc who is a super nice guy. Our water heater went out. I don't know what happened; it just stopped working. I called Marc, and he told me he'd squeeze me in. He came to the house and, with some effort, got the pilot back on. He told me I'd need a new water heater. We have a big house with a seventy-five-gallon water heater. He said that we didn't really need a seventy-five-gallon unit; a fifty-gallon unit would be cheaper and would do the job. I appreciated this; he was anticipating my cost question. He didn't have the water heater; he told me he'd order it and would call me by the end of the day to schedule installation. He did just that, then came out and installed the new water heater, and all was good.

Timing—this included the fact that he couldn't do it right away because the water heater had to be ordered from a plumbing supply house. He told me when he would call me, and he did that. He came back within a week, even though the old unit was still working, and installed the new unit. Price—he gave me options. Quality—he explained the quality of the new water heater and told me how long I could expect it to last (nothing lasts as long as it used to).

Car repair is a service where the price is normally agreed upon up front as part of the specific repair or maintenance services that are agreed to be provided. The client then has one remaining question, "When will my car be ready?"

Everyone has a car repair horror story, and I have many over many decades of owning and driving cars. I knew that I'd run over something on the San Diego Freeway and damaged some part of the car that was causing oil to leak out. I got to the dealer when they opened at 7:00 a.m. so I could get a loaner car and get my car in line to be repaired. The service writer seemed to be a competent person who told me that they'd check the car out and that he'd call me later that afternoon to let me know what was required and how long things would take. I didn't hear back from the service writer, and I knew that their service department closed at 6:00 p.m. I was good, I had a loaner car, but I was also curious as to what happened to my car and how much it would cost to repair. At about 5:30 p.m., I decided to call. "I was just about to call you," the service writer said. He explained that they needed to order some parts and that they expected to get the parts the following day and possibly have the car done the next day. And he also told me the bad news that it would cost $2,000. He concluded the conversation by telling me that I'd hear from him the next day.

Now, I know that telling someone that they have a $2,000 repair bill might be concerning for an auto repair organization. Perhaps that's why the service writer didn't want to talk to me, because, on day two, I didn't hear from him. Again, at 5:30, I called, and I got the same response—"I was just about to call you." I had not believed it when he said that the prior day. Nevertheless, the news he provided was that they didn't get the parts in a timely manner, and the car would not be ready until day three. He told me that it would be ready by noon and that he would call me.

On day three, noon came and went with no communication. Following what was now a familiar pattern, I called at 2:00 p.m., and, yes, the service writer was "just about to call me." He proudly pronounced that the mechanics were done with my car and that they were washing it as we spoke, with a commitment to have it ready in thirty minutes. I waited until 4:00 p.m., went over to the dealer's service shop, and walked in the door. The service writer saw me from across the room, looked at me, and said, "Hey, Dennis. Good to see you." All I could think was that at least he'd gotten the first letter of my name right. And, of course, the car was not yet ready. I waited another thirty minutes, and they finally brought it to me.

I survived this transaction. I even went back one more time to have an oil change. The service quality was great. The car has been fantastic. The bad experience of that one transaction left me with a negative narrative for this car dealer's service department. The car worked fine. My negative experience had nothing to do with the mechanics who repaired the car. I just couldn't get over the service writer's lack of communication. It was just this one person. I'd never worked with them prior to this and didn't work with them when I took my car back. I just lost trust that they would be able to successfully communicate with me in any future transaction more complicated than an oil change.

That is exactly what happens when the narrative is filled in by the client. Their narrative, in the absence of any other information, is going to be negative, and it's going to be negative about your organization. Clients don't ascribe blame to themselves even if they do own some of the blame. If things go wrong and you aren't communicating, you'll lose a client.

Delivering News

Let's go back to the service writer at the car dealer that we were just talking about. Why did he not call me? Was he too busy? That's his company's problem. If these guys are too busy, they have an operational problem that they need to fix. Was he afraid to give me bad news? Maybe. On day one, it was price. On day two, it was delay, so maybe he just didn't want to deliver bad news. Excellent communication includes the delivery of news—both good and bad. Yes, someone could get upset. I can guarantee that they will be more upset if they get the bad news and it's delivered in an untimely manner.

We engineers tend to do that with our clients. They don't like bad news, so we delay delivery until the "right time." That delayed delivery is, by definition, the wrong time. Tell your clients the bad news. Tell them how it impacts price, quality, and schedule. Don't wait to solve the problem before you tell them the problem. Tell them you are working on solving the problem and then keep them informed on a continuous basis. You don't have to text them three times an hour; just let them know about good developments, and every four to eight hours, if nothing has changed, let them know you are still working on it.

Communication of news requires honesty. One of the hardest things we can do is to deliver bad news to our clients. It feels like we are admitting failure or letting someone down. We're afraid it might harm our relationship or they might not like us. Delivery of bad news can be stressful and uncomfortable.

Progress reports are one mechanism for delivering news that something has changed. Had my service writer friend called me with an update on timing or cost, I would have been fine. Car repair is a service where changes can be expected. I simply wanted honesty from him, and that's not what I got.

Bad news is not like wine. It doesn't get any better with age. We'll dig into ways that you can prepare yourself to deliver bad news a bit further along in this chapter. Great communication is an art form that is beautiful to behold.

A great example of this is a guy named Victor, whose job it was to deliver a new electric vehicle to me. He has the personality of a great salesperson—friendly, happy, positive. He's knowledgeable about the car and did a good job describing it to us and sending us on our way. I'd owned the vehicle for six days when a part broke. It was no big deal but something I wanted to fix. I contacted the company's service and was sent a "service claim number." Nothing happened. I went to a certified repair shop about a forty-five-minute drive from my house, and the guy there told me he'd try to find the part and might have some idea later that day on the lead time for that part; he told me he'd give me a call (he never did).

Then I called Victor. He was unavailable but returned the call within fifteen minutes. I described the problem, and within six days, he was able to send a service guy to my house, and it was fixed. He texted me when he had good news, and he texted me when he had no news except to say he was still working on it. He texted me that I would be getting a call, but not until Tuesday, because Monday was a holiday. That's all I needed. It might have been a little bit of overkill on his part, but for me, it was perfect.

News is not always good or bad. Sometimes there is no news, and that's the place where most people struggle. No news seems like failure to us. We haven't advanced something along far enough that we can give a positive progress report, so we feel like we have failed. Put yourself in your client's shoes. When they don't know what's going on, what do they do? People need to fill in the blanks; they fill in the narrative, and it's almost always negative.

When you report "no news" to your client, you are telling them that you haven't forgotten them. You are saying you are still engaged in solving their issue or getting the promised services completed. You are saying that you are on their side and working to deliver. The next step for you is to push your organization to actually deliver what was promised to the client, or the "no news" will quickly become "bad news."

Communicate the good news, communicate the bad news, and make sure you manage the narrative by communicating when there is no news.

Delivering Bad News

No one really likes to deliver bad news, as we have already discussed. There are a few ways you can do this, with honesty, that your client may appreciate.

1. *Be honest.* Most clients expect that the person delivering bad news will be less than fully truthful. They'll sense that the bad news deliverer will be sugarcoating an issue, being overly optimistic as to the timing and cost of the solution, and perhaps just flat-out lying about the problem. The only way around this is stark, basic honesty. If you aren't prepared to be honest with your client, then you should be prepared to lose them as a client.

2. *Get prepared.* The greatest speakers in the world got that way because they were well prepared. Sir Winston Churchill was once asked to give an impromptu speech, and his response was that if the speech was to be two hours in length, he was ready to go, but if the speech was to be ten minutes in length, he would need several days to prepare. The same goes for delivering bad news to your client in a cogent and sincere manner. Think about what you are going to say and get prepared before you say it.

3. *Don't make excuses.* The client doesn't care if your supply chain has broken down or if your paint guy is out sick. Excuses make you look like you are incapable of managing your organization to deliver their promised products or services to the customer. Are you capable? Or incapable?

4. *Apologize.* It is not a sign of weakness to apologize for the failure of your organization to deliver on a commitment. People appreciate heartfelt apologies.

5. *Have a solution.* If possible, offer a solution, or a series of alternate solutions to your client. "This is how we'd like to fix things" or "This is how we will make things right" are two ways to do this. At a minimum, tell them that you are developing a solution

and let them know when you'll get back to them with a solution. And then do it!

6. *Stick with it.* Stick with things until you have a conclusion—a sale, a successful provision of services, or worst case, the client fires you.

Explanations

People have just enough attention span to listen to a message that is simply and succinctly delivered. The ability to get to the point and to make it understandable is difficult, and it is really noticeable when listening to the delivery of technical information. Explanations are about issues in not meeting client needs. They are also about explaining your product or service to your client. Often, there is a need to explain some technical aspect or some performance aspect of the product or service. This is where explanations come in.

We all know the person who once they start talking can't stop. I had a work colleague who felt most comfortable when filling nanoseconds of silence with their voice expounding on their technical expertise. This individual would speak a paragraph full of technical jargon before taking a breath. They would follow this short pause with the phrase "and so …" signifying that another paragraph's worth of jargon was about to spill out of their mouth. To my chagrin, and to the horror of our client, this also meant that we were in store for another three to five minutes of unintelligible gibberish.

We all have opportunities to talk—in person, in online meetings, in phone calls. When one goes into the "and so" mode, they often don't notice (particularly in virtual or telephone meetings) the looks of surprise on the faces of the audience. Some listeners will even be shooting lightning bolts out of their eyes at you, trying to get you to wrap it up. They thought you were about to stop, and now they only see a dark desert highway pouring out well beyond the horizon. You think the looks of amazement are due to your dazzling display of verbal wizardry; those are really the faces of despair and disappointment. On the inside, they are screaming, "Please make it stop."

In the movie *Amadeus*, the emperor is trying to explain to Mozart why he yawned very publicly and loudly during the initial public performance of an opera. I'm no music critic, and Emperor Joseph II of Austria wasn't one either. The only thing he could say about Mozart's lengthy and slightly self-indulgent composition was "Too many notes." He yawned because he lost interest as the opera labored on.

That is an apt metaphor for "overexplaining." We speak "too many notes," and we lose our audience. Simply put, overexplaining is talking too much. If you are in sales, you may have had training that instructed you to stop selling once you have made the sale so that you can stop overselling and overexplaining. It can be very irritating, and overselling can cause you to lose the sale. When someone talking to you goes into overexplaining mode, you say to yourself, "I'll never get those five minutes of my life back." That's it. You know what it is, and unless you are a very patient, kindhearted person, you'll be irritated by it.

There are many reasons that people overexplain. Here are just a few:

- *History.* You get a history lesson on the topic being discussed because they feel you need some extra context. Your client probably doesn't need to know the history of your product, service, or company.
- *Boasting.* This may occur when an opportunity arises for someone to show off their depth of knowledge of the subject matter. In the engineering world, this manifests as someone discussing a technical topic and then dropping names of dudes from the seventeenth and eighteenth centuries who have equations named after them, like Bernoulli, Pascal, and Newton. This usually doesn't leave a positive impression with your clients.
- *Gossip.* Talking to others is an opportunity to share a different kind of knowledge, gossip. Normally, this is unnecessary to reinforce any business-related point you may be trying to make. I know that office gossips can be very popular, and I can also

share with you that I do not know anyone who was an office gossip who became a senior executive. It's a pathway to nonpromotional job stasis.

- *Name-dropping.* Your client doesn't care who you know. They probably don't know the people you are talking about in an effort to be impressive. Often, I've found people gossiping to me about individuals they think I know but that I don't know. It's just another way of being boastful.

- *Lack of opportunities.* Some people overexplain as a way of staying on stage or staying in the spotlight. We've all seen the individual who needed forty-five minutes to deliver ten minutes' worth of information. If you like to talk so much, think about changing careers.

- *Lack of expertise.* Often overexplainers try to mask their lack of expertise by telling you more than you need to hear. This could be a lack of confidence in themselves or truly a lack of expertise. The more they talk, the less likely it is that they know what they are talking about. The more they talk, the more they reveal their lack of confidence in their communication skills.

- *Unprepared people don't know when to stop.* My firm was asked to give a presentation to a client in a competitive situation for a project. I helped prepare the team and actually went to the presentation, which was scheduled between 11:00 a.m. and noon. Following the presentation, the client asked our proposed project manager if he had anything else he'd like to add. This poor guy was caught off guard and assumed he should be adding something. He started talking and launched into a stream-of-consciousness-like speech that he had not, heretofore, practiced. Our hero went on for several minutes (it seemed like an eternity), and I could tell that he had no idea how to bring this thing in for a landing, so he just stopped (also known as crashing and burning), and we were done. We didn't get the job, and the one thing I will never forget is the look of astonishment and dismay on the clients' faces as my colleague spun around in outer space like Sputnik missing reentry into the earth's atmosphere. We were literally eating into their lunchtime. Bad move.

There are a few things to do to that may help you stop overexplaining.

- *Know your audience.* You need to understand your audience to deliver a crisp message. This will guide you to explain where necessary and not overexplain where it is unnecessary. You shouldn't have to explain accounting principles to a group of accountants. Nothing more needs to be said here.
- *Prepare.* We've talked about this already. Just take the time to prepare.
- *Know your subject matter.* If you are asked to speak on a topic, you had better know that topic very well and be really confident in what you are saying. Some people with a limited range of acting skills will try to come across as knowledgeable and confident. That sometimes works, but when asked a technical question, our would-be thespian often cracks because they are unable to confidently answer. Know what you are talking about or don't talk about it. Don't be a phony. Even if you do confidently understand your subject matter, you may be asked a question that you can't answer. Don't fake it. Just reply that you will strive find the answer and then talk with someone who can help you provide the answer to your client.
- *Minimize the jargon, jokes, and metaphors.* I love these. I love goofy jargon, hipster lingo, and big multisyllabic words that sound like they are a big German combo word but are really English. I like to make jokes, and when I get nervous, I tend to say what comes into my head, which may or may not be a good thing. And I love metaphors and using movie lines or lines from songs to make a point. All of this depends on your audience. These are fine in very limited dosages. Sometimes, the best thing is to just leave this stuff out, so your client doesn't get overdose on your inapt metaphors. I worked with two people who used

these to an extreme level. One loved to use movie lines and metaphors, and the other insisted on technical jargon. The technical jargon guy was just a flat-out phony. He knew the lingo, but he seemed unable to do anything but talk. He couldn't write anything; he couldn't engage with clients; he couldn't engage with our staff. All he could do is make speeches using indecipherable jargon. He had to explain what he was trying to explain. My other colleague loved movie lines and metaphors. He really liked gangster movies (*Casino, Goodfellas, The Godfather*, etc.), but he was also pretty good with any popular pop-culture phenomenon. He could quote lines from a wide variety of sources—K-pop songs to Broadway musicals like *Hamilton*. He peppered his speech with these at all opportunities. Yes, they usually got a chuckle from the audience, but I can also tell you that most in the audience had no idea what he was talking about. On occasion, a client would ask him what he meant, but most were too ashamed to out themselves with respect to their lack of familiarity with the latest Lady Gaga song, so they didn't speak up. Save the jargon and metaphors for a late-night session in the bar at your next corporate retreat and keep them away from clients.

Excuses

Excuses are as old as time itself. Just after God created Adam and Eve, they both came up with excuses. Eve said, "The devil made me do it," and Adam blamed Eve. Two people on the entire planet, and no one willing to take responsibility for a purloined apple. Even the crazy excuse that was the punch line of the 1950's vintage comedy sketch, "The dog ate my homework," actually goes back to the eighth century and can be attributed to a guy named Saint Cirian (assuming Wikipedia can be trusted).

We all make excuses, and we make them as a means of justifying bad behavior or failing at something, such as not fulfilling somebody's expectations. They can be used as a reason to not try something or as a reason to not do something. They can be used for tardiness, overspending, lack of attention, forgetfulness, inappropriate behavior, and the list can go on and on. We make excuses, and if we are honest with ourselves, we make them often.

The bottom line for you and your clients is, did you meet their expectations? When you failed to deliver on these expectations, did you say a bunch of garbage as a reason that you did not meet their expectations? Or did you simply apologize? You will invariably fall short of your clients' expectations or your contractual obligations, because you are, in fact, a fallible human being who just can't be 100 percent perfect 100 percent of the time. Like all other human beings, I've fallen short on expectations, and I've offered up some wicked stupid excuses over my multiple decades on this planet. I've also heard quite a few extraordinarily lame excuses in my official capacity as a human being, and several that I heard recently led me to think about the general category called "excuses."

We should (this may be superfluous, but I'll say it anyway) just do our jobs and meet our obligations to our clients (and our family, friends, etc.). Stuff happens, and sometimes you just can't meet an obligation. What then might be your approach to the situation, such that the first thing out of your mouth is not a lame excuse?

Let's first consider what might be going through the other person's head when we feel the big excuse welling up from within our souls and working its way out of our mouths. What are people thinking when you start to make an excuse? The first thing that pops into their head is usually something like "OK, here it comes." The "it" that's coming isn't a soft summer breeze; rather, they are referring to the whirlwind of words exiting the excuse-maker's mouth. The reality is that our excuses are often an insult to the listener. They ring of untruth or embellishment. They sound like a part of a comedy sketch that no one found funny.

In almost every instance, excuses just don't work, and they don't defuse tense situations that arise from our failure to meet an obligation. They often serve to escalate the tension and make people angrier. Our excuses tell the listener that they were less important than some other client or that the quality of the product they paid for is variable; sometimes you win, and sometimes you have to return it because it's no good. You think you are making things right with your client while offering your excuse, and in reality, you're just making them mad. They are thinking about finding another service provider or another store where they hope people can meet their obligations and get things right. The crazy thing is that they probably aren't listening to you; they are thinking of going somewhere else while you are blathering on with your funny little story about the freeway on-ramp that was blocked for tree maintenance and caused you to be late, or the time another person got upset because the product was substandard.

Your excuses for your failure or poor performance only serve to assuage your guilt—if that. The client doesn't want to buy your excuse. When you think about it, that client, like every other human being alive on our planet, has probably made the same excuse, so you really aren't fooling anyone.

Apologies

There is something that's better than an excuse. An apology is better than a lame excuse. Actually, a properly delivered and relatively sincere apology is better than a lame excuse. It's useful to explore what it is about apologies that makes them better than excuses.

- *Apologies acknowledge the issue.* "Hey, Ms. Client, it was me, not you, who messed up." You recognize what is required of you and that you did not meet that requirement. You are taking the blame.
- *Apologies are relational.* They can repair relationships, and lots of businesses are about relationships, so try to use this as an opportunity to repair the relationship with your client.

It is worth saying that an apology is not an admission, on your part, that you are inadequate as a person. It is simply an admission that, in this very specific instance, your product or service did not meet expectations or obligations. Apologies can be very tough, especially when a client or a boss is crazy mad at you. The reality is that an excuse makes someone much angrier than a sincere apology.

Apologies are not easy. It's a good idea to have a framework for offering your apology. It should not, however, be a well-rehearsed speech. The framework is a way to focus on what is important and how to move beyond the issue at hand in a positive way for you and your client. Here's a formula for handling apologies that you may consider using. It even has a little place where you can, if you really must, offer your excuse!

1. When you stepped in it, the first thing you should think about is how you will fix it going forward. What specific things will you do to finish the project, fix the product, or make things right? Think about schedule, budget, and quality. What are you going to do to at least try to make your client less angry?

2. We all like to look for someone to blame when something doesn't go right. If a client is complaining to you, you need to accept the blame. That doesn't mean you were the reason there is a problem; you are accepting the blame on behalf of your company. You can figure out who to blame later, but you have to take responsibility and get things squared away with your customer, or they will be a *former* customer. On the other hand, if you are the reason there's a problem, you should simply own it.

3. If you feel like an explanation is necessary, make your explanation short and to the point. No need to give a history of the highway system in the US if you got stuck in rush hour traffic because you overslept. The explanation—you overslept.

4. Acknowledge whatever you did wrong. I was late. The product is not up to standards. We should have done a better job on the report. Your shirt does have a stain on it that we failed to get

out. And on and on. You know that when you tell someone you are sorry, they want to know what you are sorry for.

5. Now comes the actual apology. Apologize. "I apologize that ..." Be specific. I apologize that I was late, that the product is inferior, that we didn't meet your expectations. Recognize that the issue is an inconvenience for the client. I apologize that the product is not up to standards and that you had to make an extra trip today to return it. You may have seen, from time to time, a sign on a broken elevator in a building that says, "Elevator is out of service. We are sorry for any inconvenience this may have caused." That's a lousy apology. Of course it's inconvenient. One fewer elevator means more waiting time. If you're a character in the TV sitcom *The Office*, it means you have to walk up and down a flight of stairs. Yes, it's an inconvenience. Just acknowledge that.

6. Now you can make your short explanation (recognizing that this is mostly making you feel better but not doing anything for your client) and also tell the client why it won't happen again.

7. Move forward. This is where you can talk about point number one as noted above—propose a way to fix things. We'll get you a new product. We'll fix the report. I'll get two alarm clocks so I'm never late for an early-morning meeting ever again. That's much more important to your client than your excuse. If the elevator is out of service, maybe you should commit to entering into a preventive maintenance program so you don't have unplanned outages. And if that outage occurs, perhaps you should be offering free doughnuts to give people the sugar high necessary to ascend the stairs.

8. Do what you said you would do when you said you would do it and get back to the client or customer to let them know.

Now you've closed the loop on your product or service issue. No more feeble excuses. No more dogs eating homework. No more substandard products. No more unexpected traffic while driving from suburbia to the big city. We all try to keep our promises and meet our obligations. When stuff happens, don't start with an excuse. Start with an apology, followed by a solution. You'll have more satisfied clients, and you will differentiate your organization in a very positive way.

Communicate in a way that works for your client. Don't leave gaps that force the client to make up their own negative narrative about your business interaction. Keep people informed with good news, bad news, and no news. Be honest, don't talk too much, and don't make excuses. Use communication to build trust.

A–Attention

The best way to characterize paying attention to your clients is to use the word *empathy*. Can you put yourself in your client's shoes? If you were the client, how would you like to be treated? Can you understand how they might be feeling or what they might be thinking? If you can, you are empathetic. Let's dig into this a bit more and talk about specific ways you can be empathetic.

There are a lot of details in empathy, and paying attention to someone is just the start. We'll talk about a few specific things you can do to demonstrate that you are paying attention to a client. We'll also cite some additional resources you might use to help you get better at being empathetic.

Acknowledge

One of the basics of communication is to acknowledge a client. We started discussing this in the "Communication" section, and we'll continue the discussion here because, like we said, it's a way of acknowledging someone. Acknowledgment is a basic human need. Acknowledgment also tells the client that the person greeting them (I switched from acknowledgment to greeting because I got tired of mistyping the word acknowledgment!) is socially aware, inclusive, and gracious.

We, as human beings, are appreciative when others acknowledge our existence. Greeting clients in retail settings is simply a gracious thing to do. Some businesses have their employees say things like "Welcome in" or "Welcome to (insert name of business here)." That's fine if that's your brand. You may be surprised to hear that, to most of us, the shouted "Welcome to (name of business)!" seems trite. Perhaps the easiest thing is a simple hello.

On a recent visit to the local coffee hangout (to work on the book), the young hipster in the goldenrod-colored, knit cap immediately greeted me with a "Hello, sir."

I replied with a "Good morning" and then followed that up with "Sir? What prompted you to call me sir?"

"Well," he replied, "you just look like a sir, and I thought that I would recognize your sir-ness." It's tough to beat that response. I was dressed in my teaching garb—dress shirt, fancy jeans, nice shoes. I also have the right hair color (or noncolor) to be a member of the sir class. It was the greeting that mattered, and I can't really do anything about my hair color without looking like I'm trying too hard to look younger.

People want to be acknowledged. Doing this in a pleasant manner that doesn't seem trite can be memorable, and that's one way of creating a better experience. The young hipster got it right.

Look People in the Eye

The disembodied voice called out from some hidden location, "Hey! Welcome in!" It was pleasant, it was timely, and it was not connected to any human being I could see. Eye contact is a big part of acknowledgment. There are lots of scientific studies that look at how the brain reacts to eye contact. Mostly, these reactions are very positive, although extended eye contact can, I think we would all agree, be weird.

Business transactions are, to state the obvious, not intended to be confused or conflated with any aspect of arousal. Eye contact is part of acknowledgment but not everywhere. This discussion is really limited to Western cultures, where eye contact is a form of respect.

In a typical business interaction, we often don't think about eye contact. I don't make a lot of eye contact with the dentist when she is drilling out a tooth. In fact, I prefer that she focus on the task at hand. I do, on the other hand, want the accountant or lawyer looking at me when we are talking. Eye contact is a form of acknowledgment of someone's presence and status.

In a retail setting, I am looking for eye contact. I feel that the person who is willing to acknowledge me is also likely to pay attention to me and help me find exactly what I am looking for. That may or may not be true. The disembodied voice might also be able to direct me to the appropriate location in the store or provide some advice as I try to sort through options. It gets the job done. It just doesn't get it done at any level that leads to a positive experience.

You may be interested to know that the portions of the brain, shown by research, to react to eye contact include those areas that process working memory, decision-making, mood regulation, timing, and novelty detection. Some of these are probably relevant to a business interaction. I would like to positively influence decision-making in the favor of my product or service. Timing is probably an interesting one as well, as we'd like the client to make a decision for our product sooner rather than later. Mood regulation may not impact the overall purchase decision, but I think it would be a good thing if a client left my store in a good mood rather than a foul one.

One thing you should not do is stare at the other person. Don't lock in on their eyes in an unwavering, bad-guy-in-a-gangster-movie kind of way. A general rule of thumb is to make eye contact while conversing with someone for 50 percent to 75 percent of the time. The rest of the time, you can look up, down, or to the side. You want to show acknowledgment and respect, not convey fear.

If you want to compete, perhaps the higher level of acknowledgment and respect will differentiate you from your competitors and maybe even earn you more clients who are committed to your brand.

The Story

The overwhelming predisposition of someone interacting with a potential client is to start pitching your product or service. We want our prospective client to know all about what we can do for them and how we can make their lives *so* much better. Then we want to tell them about our own experience with the product or service to provide the social proof that what we are offering to them is the best—the *best*!

All of this may be true. We may have the best product. It may indeed make the client's life significantly better. They won't believe it. They'll feel like they are being pushed into making a decision. They won't be sure they can trust you. One of the reasons for this is you haven't taken the time to learn their story.

We made an appointment for someone to come to our home to discuss upgrading our air-conditioning system. This individual texted us that he was on his way and would arrive at the agreed-upon time. He included in his text a fairly lengthy bio about himself that had nothing to do with air-conditioning and more to do with his golf game.

He was doing so well—communicating with us about his arrival time, being responsive by showing up at the agreed-upon time. He was paying attention as well, but he was paying attention to himself, not to us. He was telling us his story, and that really had nothing to do with air-conditioning systems.

What is the client's story? It's definitely not their full life history, and it's not anything personal. It's what are they trying to achieve. What do they want from the service or product that you are offering? What is important to them? What will frame their purchase decision? They want to know that you are on their team, trying to help them make a good decision. They want to know that you care about them. As mentioned earlier, Theodore Roosevelt, the twenty-sixth president of the United States, said, "People don't care how much you know until they know how much you care."

You do this by asking simple, nonintrusive questions. You want to know the prospective client's story so that you can figure out how your product or service fits into their story. They talk; you listen. This seems like a no-brainer, but for many people, it's hard to do.

I had a problem with my foot, and I was referred to an orthopedic surgery practice. As is my usual routine, I did some research to see where the doctors in this practice had gone to college and medical school, and where they had gained experience. One doctor caught my eye: Stanford Medical School and some experience serving as one of the team doctors for the Stanford football team and one of the local professional football teams. I made an appointment to visit this doctor, who examined my foot and presented to me options for fixing the problem. He asked me, "What's driving you? Do you want to fix this as quickly as possible (which required a surgical intervention), or do you want to take your time with some prosthetics, which may or may not fix the problem?"

It was October, and ski season was coming quickly. "I've got an annual ski pass, and I'm planning on using it in December, so I want to get back on the field as soon as possible," I told him. I had the surgery the next week and was skiing with my sons in December.

This doctor figured out what I was about. He listened to my story. He didn't need to tell me his story. I'd already figured that out; that's why I was there in the first place. For the record, I told him this up front. The only remaining thing was the story of the service. There were only two things I cared about relative to the service. Will this fix my problem? Yes, permanently. Will I be full bore on the ski slopes in December? Yes, mid-December at the latest. This practitioner understood my story, had the right service, and delivered an excellent experience.

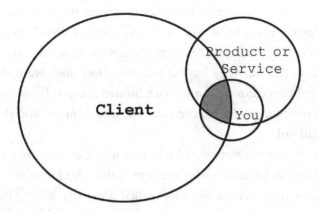

Figure 4. The focus of your attention

One way to look at this is shown graphically in figure 4. The focus of your attention has to be on the client, not on your product/service and definitely not on you. This surgeon might have delivered to me a monologue about the athletes he'd treated or his excellent education at Stanford. I would have politely listened, but I would have wondered if I was just a number to him—another dude with a physical problem that he could fix by engaging his amazing intellect and highly honed skills. Just another notch on his belt.

He made my story the focus of his attention. That's what we need to do if we are really paying attention to our clients.

Anticipate–Don't Coagulate

We often think we know what customers want. We decide that we know what they are looking for or what their thought process might be in making a purchase decision. While you might be anticipating how a potential client will behave, you are also likely coagulating around your best guess as to how they will behave. Sometimes you're right, and sometimes you're wrong. Being wrong isn't necessarily a deal killer, but it makes the sales hill tougher to climb.

Think about your interaction with a client as a soft negotiation.

This isn't a zero-sum game where there is a winner and a loser; rather, it's an interaction where you try to achieve a win for the client, which is a de facto win for you and your company. Negotiators always want the other side to feel like they have autonomy. They don't want the other party to feel backed into a corner with limited choices. If you coagulate around a position, you've backed someone into a corner, and that often leads to fail-fail.

There is a sports metaphor I like that might explain this. It has to do with English football—what we here in the USA know as soccer.

There is, in soccer, a situation called a penalty kick. The ball is placed on the penalty spot, twelve yards from the goal line. The goalkeeper, who is attempting to stop the shot from going in the goal, is positioned at the goal line and may not move until the ball is kicked by the player from the opposing team who is taking the penalty shot. Penalty shots are notoriously very difficult to stop, but sometimes the goalkeeper does actually make the save and deny the goal to the opposing team.

The general strategy that the goalkeeper makes is to anticipate where the opposing player may kick the ball and then to dive in that direction to attempt to stop the shot. Goalkeepers normally dive to their left or their right, and sometimes they stay in the middle. Even if they guess correctly, a skilled shot taker may put the ball past the goalkeeper and into the net. In effect, the goalkeeper must coagulate around their anticipation with respect to the direction of the shot. There is no second chance; either they are right, and they might stop the shot, or they are wrong, and the penalty kick is successful, which is bad for the goalkeeper's team on the whole. In fact, goalkeepers successfully block around 11 percent of penalty kicks taken. That's not a very good record.

If you are trying to anticipate a client's purchasing behavior, you'll likely have a higher success rate than soccer goalkeepers. You will also likely get a second chance if you are wrong in your first attempt. Sometimes people don't take advantage of their second chance because they are so locked into their initial assumptions that they don't know how to shift their mental model of the potential client. That's a goal for the other guys.

Most of us aren't professional athletes. Our decisions don't cause elation or depression for our fan base when we are right or we are wrong. We're just trying to take care of a client. Sometimes we guess right, and sometimes we guess wrong. I'll give two more examples.

My client in Utah was getting ready to build a large facility that had been engineered by my company. One day, prior to a monthly board meeting at the headquarters of his public agency, he expressed some concern with respect to using the traditional method of procuring a construction contractor. This method awards the construction project to the lowest bid price submitted by a competent construction contractor. I advised the client that there were alternatives to this method and that my company had experience with several of these alternatives.

I started to explain what I knew about the different alternatives because I was sure that my client wanted to hear my copious knowledge about the topic. (Just kidding here. I had very limited knowledge of this particular topic.) I had anticipated that he might have this concern and had prepared to tell him as much as I knew. Most clients would have let me do this. My anticipated position was that my Utah client would let me do some "engineer-splaining" of this topic.

His body language was no bueno. I'm a lousy body language reader, but if someone makes it really obvious, I can tell what they are thinking. I knew he didn't want to hear it from me. I shifted gears and offered to bring in the president of our construction company to describe the various alternatives. The client looked at me and said, "Good answer, because I know you really don't know much about this topic." He was right. I wondered how he knew this. I was grateful that his body language was obvious. The president of our construction company did a fantastic job clearly explaining the alternatives to the client. This ultimately led to a nice construction contract for my company.

Anticipation—check. Preparation—check. Coagulating around the anticipated reaction—no. Building trust with the client and making a sale—yes.

You may have experienced a salesperson shifting away from an initial position. This happened to me in the Tiffany's jewelry store in Pasadena, California. I went in after work one night, wearing the suit and tie that I had been wearing during the day. Most people in the store were dressed casually. I stood out simply because I had on nice business attire. I came to buy a gift for a family member. A salesperson offered to assist me. I told her what I was about, and she began to show me some very expensive items. I understand that this is a typical way of selling luxury items. Start at the top and work your way down. This gives the client a reference with respect to prices and often results in the psychological effect for the buyer that they are getting a good deal on the lower-priced items. The salesperson could see instantly that she'd overreached—by a lot. I love my family, but a $10,000 necklace is more of an inheritance than a birthday gift. The salesperson then showed me some items that were several price notches below the initial items, and I was able to select some nice, reasonably priced (for Tiffany's) items, and all parties were happy.

Did this person anticipate what I might be interested in? Absolutely, yes. Did she then adjust her strategy and approach immediately after getting an initial negative reaction? Yes, she did. She made my visit to Tiffany's a fun and memorable experience, and she also got credit for a sale!

Body Language

Body language might be the holy grail of business. The ability to read another person's body language *and* to convey information through your body language would be phenomenal. I'd love to be an expert in either one of these skill sets. Like any other skill, you have to practice, practice, and practice some more if you want to get good at it. Even then, you won't be right all the time because someone can behave a certain way or display specific body language that is unintentional, leading you to misinterpret what might be in their head.

As an example, a work colleague asks you, "Are you even listening to me?" They ask this because you are not looking at them, you didn't smile or laugh when they told you their funny story, and you are staring into space. Most of those body language identifiers say that you weren't listening. Yet perhaps you were listening to them and simply chose not to look at them as they were speaking, and you didn't think that their story was funny. Or perhaps you had something else on your mind, and your lack of attention had nothing to do with the work colleague; it was related to an issue that you were facing that was dominating your brain at that particular moment in the day.

You can't see into someone's brain. You can only try to guess what's going on inside their cranium, based on some outward body language identifiers. Here are a few for you to consider. There is a quote from the movie *Anchorman* that is quite apt for reading body language. In the movie, one of the characters invents a cologne called Sex Panther. His tagline for the cologne is "Sixty percent of the time, it works every time!" This is also true for body language readers; most of the time, you'll be right, but not every time, so keep that in mind.

Eyes—we're right back at the eyes thing. Shakespeare said, "The eyes are the window to your soul." That is very true because there are parts of your eyes that you cannot control. We don't control our pupils, and these can potentially tell a story. In any case, this offers another good reason for you to look people in the eye. Here are some of the things that the eyes can tell us:

- If someone is looking at you while you are talking, they are most likely paying attention to what you are saying. I realize this seems obvious.
- If someone is trying to stare you down, they are often trying to intimidate you or control the situation. This has happened to me numerous times. Once, while making a sales presentation in the Middle East, the leader of the client team, who was a high-ranking government official, had me in a death stare. While I was talking, he was staring at me; while others were talking, he was staring at me. It was weird, and it was

very intimidating. I didn't want to stare back at him, so I very self-consciously "acted natural." He was definitely trying to intimidate me to see if I would crack. Thankfully, I had no idea what he was doing, so I kept my cool.

- The pupils. If someone's pupils are widening (remember, we can't control our pupils), it might mean that they are happy and interested in what you are saying. If their pupils are narrowing, it might mean that they are concerned or unhappy.

- Abnormal blinking. This usually is a sign of discomfort. What that may mean in a business interaction can be a lot of different things. You might want to ask the client if they are OK with continuing the conversation.

- Avoiding eye contact. Normally this is a sign of disinterest or boredom. For many, it's the unspoken way of saying, "Leave me alone." It could also be a sign of shyness. Those of us who are pathological introverts are more comfortable staring at our own shoes than at someone who is speaking to us.

The head and face tell us a lot about someone. The most obvious is if someone is smiling. We all know what that means, and, in most cases, it means what you think it means; they are interested in what you have to say or want you to help them. Just remember, not always. Here are some other ways that the head and face can inform us:

- Faces are expressive. The following emotions (and this is not a comprehensive list) are often expressed and can be pretty easily identified: happiness, sadness, fear, excitement, contempt, satisfaction, boredom, and many more. You do not need to be a body language expert to read these signals.

- Nodding. When someone is nodding positively (up and down) while you are speaking, that's a good thing. When they are shaking their head side to side, that's a bad thing.

- People who show tension in their head or neck or are pursing their lips are concerned. They might not believe what you are telling them, or they might not want to engage with you. You can simply ask if they have any concerns or would like to be left alone.

- Turned away from you—probably a sign that they aren't paying attention or don't care what you have to say.

If someone is doing something with their hands, like drumming their fingers, cracking their knuckles, or any other fidgety-type activity, they are bored. Get to the point before you lose them. If people get out their phones when you are speaking with them, this also might indicate boredom, or it may be a sign that they have a debilitating smartphone addiction.

If someone's body and feet are pointed toward you, they are paying attention and are interested in what you are saying. If they are turned away, that's the opposite. If their feet are tapping or moving, it's the same as tapping or moving hands; they are bored.

If someone speaks with you, you can often tell if they are interested in continuing a conversation or wish to be left alone. This one is usually problematic for me because most people try to be socially polite in their interactions with others. That politeness can be misinterpreted as interest. You have to simply ask if they are interested because they won't tell you that they are not interested since they don't want to seem unkind or impolite.

Get Their Name Right!

Names are important. They are a massive part of our individual identity. We get, from our names, a sense of who we are, including personal identity, cultural identity, and familial or historical connections. People with unusual or foreign names can tell you how frustrating and off-putting it is to have their names mispronounced or misspelled. It is a significant sign of respect to get someone's name right and to use it appropriately. I'll give some personal examples, and I do not have a difficult name by any measure:

- Use their name. One of our sons had a girlfriend who refused to use my name or my wife's name. We had intentionally told her early on in their relationship that she could call us by our first names. It's just easier. She refused to do it. She would see us and say, "Hey …" with a lingering pause because—well, I don't know why. She simply couldn't say our names. and I don't think it was because she wanted to call us Mr. and Mrs.; rather, it was because she didn't really like us. ("In the absence of a narrative, people will make up their own, and it's usually negative" seems to apply here). If you know someone's name, use it whether you like them or not.

- Use their name appropriately. Has someone ever overused your name, making your name part of every sentence, sometimes using it two or three times in each sentence? It's way over the top. It's irritating. Don't do it.

- Ask them what they like to be called. Once you know someone, it's OK to ask them what they prefer to be called. I get this frequently from someone I've recently met. They'll ask me if I like to be called "Dave" or "David." My response is that I don't care—either one works for me. Others may be pickier about what they are called.

- Cut people a bit of slack. My mother-in-law sometimes called me Steve. I took it with some grace. She had four kids, all married, and loads of grandkids. It can be easy to forget someone's name. I actually didn't mind, and I found it kind of charming because Steve is the name of my brother-in-law who is married to my wife's older sister. I've known Steve since I was in middle school and have always looked up to him and admired him, so being confused for Steve wasn't necessarily a bad thing to me. I am not sure that Steve would have felt the same way if she had called him Dave.

- Foreign names. It's a small world. I live in California, and there are people from all over the world living here. Many have names that come from their country of origin. Some have names that honor their heritage. Not everyone has a good old American-sounding name. The best way to deal with this, when you hear a foreign name that you might not be able to pronounce, is to ask the individual to help you pronounce their name correctly. That's a great way to acknowledge them and show respect. Don't give them a nickname or American-ize their foreign name. I had a work colleague who had Lithuanian heritage. His name was Tiit. He pronounced it "Teet." I once asked him why he had not Americanized it, and he said, "My mother gave me this name, and changing it would have been disrespectful to her." That's good enough for me.

- Nicknames. Our coworker's husband was named "Butch." That just doesn't seem like an appropriate name for a middle-aged adult male. Is that his given name? Nope. Why doesn't he use his given name now that he is a married adult and a father? Because he hates his given name—Floyd. OK, that makes sense. People who tell you their name is Butch, or any other nickname, have a reason for doing this. Just go with the flow.

Speak Their Language

One of my colleagues liked to use the highest level of technical jargon that one could possibly imagine. Perhaps he believed that this indicated the depth of his knowledge in his are of "expertise." I often wondered if our clients understood him. No one objected to his jargon-laded mono-logues. No one asked him what he meant or asked him to define any specific terms he was using. I understood him because I had been around him enough to have a good sense of what he was talking about. I simply don't know if our clients understood him, and that was more important.

People normally don't like to let on that they don't understand some-thing. This makes me think of my high school physics class with Mr. Locheed, who was a really good teacher. There are some pretty arcane subjects in physics that, when initially introduced, can be very difficult to understand. Fortunately, we had one person in the class who was willing to ask Mr. Locheed for more information or to clarify a specific topic. This made it easier and better for all of us. That often doesn't happen in a business setting.

In business discussions or transactions, the client has a lot of things going through their head. They may not ask the right questions or ask for clarification. Again, people don't like to indicate a lack of understanding. It's incumbent upon you to figure out what "language" they speak and to tailor your discussion to their level of ability.

My jargon-heavy colleague had a terrible time with most of our clients. They simply didn't understand him and didn't appreciate what they sensed was his overcomplication of specific technical issues. The smartest people can usually figure out a way to explain complex issues in a direct, simplified, digestible manner. They can also dial up the jargon and complexity if the client is into that sort of thing. You have to be very vigilant and watch body language (as previously discussed) to make sure you are speaking their language.

My wife and I walked into a shop selling Murano glass in Stressa, Italy. The woman who was working in the shop looked up at us the instant we walked in and politely said, "Good morning," to us in unaccented English. Reminder, this is Italy. She was clearly speaking German to the other couple that was in the shop buying something. When the German-speaking transaction was completed, she came to talk with us, and I asked her how she knew we were English speakers. Her response was that she knew we were Americans from the way we were dressed and what we were carrying (I probably had a 35 mm camera over my shoulder). She told us that she had owned this shop for twenty-five years and over time had learned what different nationalities looked like, and with a very short conversation, she could tell what they were interested in buying. This is a very literal example. You can, however, learn to speak in a way that is best for your clients, to build on their experience in working with you.

Sometimes people need to carefully listen to themselves and ask if there might be an easier way to explain something or to describe some attribute of a product or service. A former mentor is one of the smartest people I've ever known. He usually could express complex concepts in clear, understandable language. He occasionally would wander off the reservation and seek the perfect words or phrases to describe something, and when he did this, it could be a problem. Yes, he had the perfect words, but they might not be terms in common usage and therefore not intelligible to his audience. Interestingly enough, many clients actually found this to be a positive because it was really an indication of how smart this individual is.

Strive for clarity. There are no Pulitzer Prizes for complicated sales pitches. The smartest people can explain complex topics using everyday language. Go for that end of the spectrum.

Listen

This could be a one-word section—*listen*. You need to listen to your clients. There are lots of books on listening. There are many listening experts and coaches. You simply need to remind your employees that their goal is to get clients to talk about themselves, the product or service that they are seeking, and what their goals are for that product or service.

Part of *attention* is paying attention to what you are doing and how you are communicating. One thing that can absolutely destroy any trust that you have with a client is manipulation. This seems like a good place to talk about ways clients might feel manipulated.

Silence has meaning, and sometimes it means no. This is something that is highly nuanced, but it bears mentioning because it exists in many business interactions. In a large meeting with one of our clients, a question was posed to the client leader by our team leader, Marty. The question posed wasn't particularly controversial, but it did require the client to commit to an action. By way of background, Marty is well liked by the client, and he appears to have a very friendly, trust-based relationship with the client leader.

The immediate response following the question was silence for about ten seconds. That is an eternity when you are waiting for an answer. Finally, the client leader said, "We'll see." I don't even know what that really means in this context. It could mean yes, no, or anything in between. I do, however, think the silence told me more than those two spoken words. I think the silence was a no, because the client leader didn't want to undermine Marty or hurt his feelings in front of Marty's team. The client leader held Marty in high regard and liked working with him, and he didn't want to insult his friend. As it turned out, the answer was no. Marty wasn't listening to the silence.

Don't Overdo It

One of life's most memorable experiences is the purchase of your first new car. It's thrilling and terrifying at once. You check prices, find a dealer that has the car you want at the price you can afford, go to the dealer, test-drive the car, decide to purchase it, and then you are run through the gauntlet of the dealer's sales machine. How will you finance the car? Do you want a special protective finish on the body or on the upholstery? Do you want an extended warranty? Do you want tire replacement insurance? And the list can continue on with several more "Do you want" opportunities for you to spend money on stuff you probably don't need. This is called upselling.

Upselling exists in just about every retail and service business.

There is a metaphorical cliff that exists in any sales transaction. Going too far can take your sale over the cliff and kill it. This section is about making a sale and not killing your client (or your sale) in the process.

Many businesses look at the acquisition of a new customer as just the start of a long and profitable (for the business) relationship. They use proven sales methods to get you to buy more stuff to go with your initial purchase. The business, of course, thinks they are doing the customer a favor by giving them options. The customer may be a bit confused. "If a special protective coating on the upholstery of my new car is a good idea, why doesn't the factory just make it a standard application for all cars?"

As a customer, I can definitely say that I don't like having to navigate this phalanx of extra options even if some of them might be useful and appropriate. Businesses know that upselling can be problematic with customers, yet they persist in this practice. This is not an empathetic response.

My wife and I purchased, at a car dealer, a used SUV with run-flat (this is important) tires. Going through the dealer's standard purchasing process, we were offered a series of extras that we rejected, politely but firmly. The finance guy then told us that there was one last option that was a fantastic deal and something I should definitely take—tire insurance. I'd never heard of this and asked about it. For $2,000, the dealer would replace any tire that failed for any reason for the duration of my ownership of the vehicle. I had my phone with me, went out to the car and looked at the tire sizes, and found them online for prices between $300 and $400 each. So, for this insurance to have value to us, at least five tires would have to fail and require replacement over the lifetime of the vehicle. If a tire just came to the end of its useful life due to tread wear, it wasn't eligible under this insurance policy. Since I can do arithmetic, I decided to not take them up on this "we're saving the best for last" offer.

This experience caused me to consider these specific questions. Why do businesses feel the need to upsell? What is it about upselling that turns people off? What can businesses do to upsell fairly and with integrity?

Why Do Businesses Upsell?

The most prominent reason is because they can. Once you've been sold the new car, the new bicycle, the new life insurance policy, or the new suit of clothes, you are a candidate for buying more stuff to go along with what you have already purchased.

If you search the internet for the term *upsell*, you'll see a long list of articles with advice on how to upsell. There are books written about it, and I think one of the best is *Influence: The Psychology of Persuasion* by Robert Cialdini. Dr. Cialdini is a professor of psychology and marketing at Arizona State University. I really like this book, and I'm definitely recommending it to you. Its concepts can be used for good, or they can be used for evil. Nevertheless, you should learn more about the seven "influencers" in Dr. Cialdini's book.

Businesses upsell because they can, and there are formulas for hooking people into buying a product or service or buying add-ons to that product or service. Buying a car is an experience we've already discussed, and you'll get similar treatment if you buy new bedroom furniture at any furniture store or a new dishwasher at Home Depot. Delivery, installation, hauling away the old stuff, new installation hardware (can't put the old electrical cord or old flexible water connectors on the new dishwasher), and extended warranty.

Businesses also do this because they make more money. Our friends at Home Depot are making a bet that your dishwasher will operate problem-free for the initial one-year warranty period and well beyond the three-year extended warranty period. That's a good bet for Home Depot because, in my experience, I can think of no occasion where a major appliance or expensive piece of electronic gadgetry failed within five years of purchasing it.

Some upsell product and service offerings may actually be beneficial and financially smart for you. I bought a used car and purchased a service warranty for oil changes and normal service because I knew how much I was going to drive the car and, doing the math, it seemed like a reasonable deal. Teeth whitening at the dentist, changing the windshield wipers when the car is in for an oil change, a retro Led Zeppelin T-shirt when buying new jeans—and more; I've been upsold a lot and generally have no regrets about it.

Just for balance, I will note that the retailers and service providers that I still go to and trust the most are the ones who have told me that I could purchase the extra service or products, but I don't really need it, and it's not something they would purchase for themselves. Upsell can make the company more money, and there are proven methodologies to get the purchaser of the goods or services to feel like they need to buy the upsell offering. It can, at times, be good for the purchaser as well, but it's not always good, and you usually don't feel too good about the process.

What Is Upsetting about Upsell?

We are going to get slightly technical here, and I am going to venture, ever so briefly and lightly, into the world of neuroeconomics. There is famous experiment called the Ultimatum Game that offers a rationale for how most people react to upselling and explains the behavior of people who feel that the upselling activity is a scam.

In the Ultimatum Game, there are two parties whose brains are hooked up to some type of *Ghostbuster*-ish brain wave–measuring device. The "adult in the room" tells both parties that they have twenty brand-new one-dollar bills. They will then proceed to give all twenty of the crisp new ones to Party No. 1.

Both parties are informed that Party No. 1 will decide how much of their newfound wealth they will share with Party No. 2. The "adult" tells both parties that Party No. 1 can share zero, one, two, ten, or any amount of one-dollar bills with Party No. 2. Party No. 2 may accept or reject the transaction. If Party No. 2 accepts, then both parties get to keep what they have in their hands. If Party No. 2 rejects the transaction, they both get nothing.

This is exciting. Who will get the rose? As it turns out, if Party No. 1 gives a small amount of their dollar bills to Party No. 2, Party No. 2 will most likely reject the transaction. If Party No. 2 receives a reasonable amount of the dollar bills, say somewhere between seven and ten, they are more likely to accept the transaction, and both parties get to keep the money in their hands.

That totally makes sense, and I think most of us would operate the same way. But why would we do this? Efficient economic theory says that if Party No. 1 gives one dollar to Party No. 2, then Party No. 2 is a dollar richer, and they should accept the transaction, notwithstanding the fact that they know that Party No. 1 was really cheap with them and kept 95 percent of the money. Party No. 2 rejects the transaction, which is, in economic theory, irrational. Here is where neuroeconomics comes into the picture. That brain wave–measuring device is there to figure out what is going on inside the brain of Party No. 2 while this financial transaction is taking place.

When Party No. 2 feels that they are being cheated because Party No. 1 didn't offer them a "fair amount" of the twenty-dollar loot, the part of the brain that allows irrational behavior supernovas. Thus, Party No. 2 does the irrational thing and rejects what they consider to be a low amount of money.

This is a long-winded way of explaining that, when people are up-sold, if they feel that someone is trying to take advantage of them or cheat them financially, they will act irrationally. You feel irrational when you think someone is selling you something you don't want or need.

Simply put, people don't like to be upsold because they feel that they are getting cheated. No one likes to be ripped off. This is particularly problematic in services where there exists a trust factor between the service provider and the client. This is tricky because it takes a long time to build trust, and it can be lost on one bad transaction. Most of us want to give people a chance, so perhaps it will take two bad transactions for us to lose trust.

My friend Don was buying a new business suit. Don is a fashionista, always well-dressed even at the company picnic. He looks like he reads GQ and actually pays attention to their advice. He decided on a particular suit and tried it on to get measured for alterations. As he reengaged with the salesperson to purchase the suit, she pushed him to purchase a shirt, necktie, and pocket square, telling him that she was a great stylist and that he would really stand out if he paired these items with his new suit. It's minor, but what irritated Don is that, had this salesperson taken a few seconds to talk with Don or even notice how he was dressed, she would have easily concluded that he was not in need of her styling help and defi-nitely did not need her proposed shirt-tie-pocket-square combo. Again, it's not a big deal, but it's also not a positive element of client experience.

There are few other things in a business transaction that irritate me more than being upsold. I don't like having my time wasted listening to an extended sales pitch for something that I'm not going to purchase. I don't like having to make decisions on smaller stuff right after I've made a big purchase decision. I don't like having to do math in my head while I'm smiling at a salesperson who I feel is trying to empty my pockets as fast as they can. I don't like being manipulated. You likely feel the same way, and you could probably add some more "don't likes" to this list.

Upselling and integrity are inextricably linked. If your client feels that they are being manipulated by you trying to upsell something to them, they will simply not be able to trust you. The way to maintain and grow a trust relationship with your client is through your ongoing demonstrated integrity. *Webster's* defines integrity as "firm adherence to a code of especially moral or artistic values: incorruptibility." Synonyms for integrity include character, decency, honesty, and morality.

Integrity can be demonstrated by service providers and by those engaged in a retail transaction. Most of us have internal lie detection meters of varying sensitivities, depending on the circumstances. If I'm buying a car, my meter is very sensitive. If I'm buying a sports drink at a convenience store, my meter is turned off. In between is the area where retailers can really care for their customers. Just assume that your client's lie detection meter is in hypersensitive mode and put yourself in their shoes. You probably won't do much upselling.

Do You See Me Now?

A Franciscan priest named Father Richard Rohr said, "Most people do not see things as they are; rather, they see things as 'they' are." In client interactions, you need to try to see things through the lens your client is seeing things, not through your particular lens. We all think we are pretty good at this; Father Rohr thinks otherwise.

Do you ever wonder why you are so often right and everyone else is wrong? You probably don't have a scorecard on this, but if you did, you'd see yourself as having a phenomenal winning record. Right and wrong; black and white; true and false—these are the prepackaged choices that exist for one who lives in a world of duality. This is a place where many of us like to live. In this world, there are only two answers, and mine is right, so I guess that leaves you as the opposite of right!

The world of duality is not a world of reality. We're not talking about religion or (dare I say it) politics. Let's stick to business because I think that will be far less upsetting to most of us. You can, of course, take it further with your morning-Zoom-coffee-clan to discuss a topic du jour like politics in Western Europe, the precise definition of a polar ice cap, or the best color to paint a bedroom. I'd like to stick to the topic of business and the decisions, personal interactions, and everyday discourse of the business world.

People live in a world that is mired in duality. As Father Rohr says, we tend to see things as we are. The problem with this is that the "we" can obscure reality. Is this a big deal in business? Yeah, because to do the best things for your business, for your employees, for your clients and customers, the answers often don't exist in a dualistic world. Most business issues are much more highly nuanced because they involve people, and people fundamentally do *not* exist on the extremes of the duality spectrum; rather, they are somewhere in between *right* and *wrong*.

We make decisions every day, and we want our decisions to be right. We are all very smart people (with all of our advanced degrees and years of experience), but better decision-making exists in a reality that's inclusive of other people's ideas and points of view that we'd not previously considered.

You can break the mold of dualistic thinking. We'll take a brief look at what's wrong with duality and how it keeps us from seeing reality. Then we'll talk about some things you might consider doing to adopt a growth mindset around business decision-making.

Duality is dismissive. A dualistic approach to business decision-making will cause you to miss every nuance that exists between the two bookends of the decision spectrum—I am right, and you are wrong. You may be doing this subconsciously, or you may be doing it purposefully. In either case, it has negative consequences.

Duality is self-limiting. You are dismissing an entire subset of information that doesn't line up with your viewpoint. Are you so certain of your analysis, viewpoint, facts, and information that you can dismiss the information brought by others? You are creating a zero-sum game, one in which there are only winners and losers, where it does not need to exist. Your paradigm of duality is very likely to miss critical information that could lead to better decision-making. That, in itself, should be reason enough for anyone to open their mind to the input of others.

Duality is a negative practice. It doesn't engender discussion or debate. General George S. Patton is credited with saying, "If everyone is thinking alike, then someone's not thinking." You are forcing, by a dualistic perspective, everyone to think like you. In so doing, you are creating a negative vibe in your workplace and with your client.

Dualistic thinkers seek others who agree with their opinions and ignore those who disagree. Duality creates a demeaning, conflict-ridden, limiting, and negative work ethos. In a world where businesses compete for the best people, a duality culture is not one that attracts the best minds.

Duality leads to overexplaining. If you think you have all the knowledge and that your client has zero knowledge, you will spew out too many words. This will cause your client to yawn.

Finally, duality is arrogant. You are suggesting that you are the touchstone of decision-making and others have no idea what they are doing unless they agree with you. Are you really that good? After many decades in the engineering and construction business, I can say with certainty that I've never met a CEO, COO, CFO, manager, supervisor, or subject matter expert who was always right. To answer my rhetorical question, *no*, you aren't that good. No one is always right.

Moving to reality, you can break free of duality by recognizing some of the things that cause it and then making a conscious, consistent effort to identify dualistic thinking and move beyond it. You won't get there overnight, but the move to reality starts with the recognition of your own personal duality.

Naïve realism. This is the sense that we see things as they really are, and it enables us to disregard any information that may challenge our thinking. We deny the existence of our personal biases and filters that may change our sense of reality. This is, stating the obvious, naïve.

Personal biases. You know that you have personal biases that lead you to think in certain ways and to make decisions in certain ways. I don't know what your issues are. I only know that you, like everyone else on this planet, have issues in your life that cause your personal biases. You may not know what biases you have. Start by recognizing that you are a biased person and then try to open your mind to others' viewpoints.

Motivated reasoning. This is a psycho term for thinking through a topic or problem with the aim, conscious or unconscious, of reaching the conclusion that we wanted to reach in the first place. This is having a discussion with your team and working to get them to all agree with you, rather than actually listening to why your reasoning may be faulty. I recently asked a client why our firm was not selected for a project, and my brain simply stopped recording data once they told me that they were upset with our project manager. This wasn't the only reason, of course, that they didn't select us. At the start of the call, I was pretty sure that this was the problem, and once the client mentioned this, I had my answer. I also missed out on some other good feedback that was probably very useful.

Training trap. Your training, both academic and professional, can skew your judgment. You may tend to disregard someone who perhaps doesn't have your academic pedigree. You may think that your vast experience gives you knowledge no one else could possibly have. To quote Dwight Schrute from the TV show *The Office*, "False." You've fallen into the training trap. Here is my own story about motivated reasoning and a training trap that really has nothing to do with business decision-making but exemplifies how these messed with me. I'm a wastewater engineer who likes to do crossword puzzles. One Sunday, I was struggling with the clue, "Old Glory sewer." I kept on thinking, *What sewer (as in pipe that carries sewage) is called the Old Glory sewer?* I figured that perhaps Washington, DC, had named a sewer pipe "Old Glory" and that it must have some other feature, function, or name that would be the answer to this crossword puzzle clue. I was really hyped that the authors of the Sunday Crossword were finally giving props to the wastewater industry and putting in a clue that only the wastewater illuminati would be able to answer. And I was way wrong on this. The answer, as 99.99 percent of the population knows, is Betsy Ross. She sewed the first flag, commonly known as "Old Glory." My training and wastewater motivation trapped me.

You can learn, and you can break the mold of dualistic thinking. You have to make a conscious effort to do this. Here are a few ways to start down the path of reality.

Learn to listen. You can ask questions in lieu of giving answers. Then you should listen to the answers that are given by your team and ask more questions. The key is to listen. Listening is not that easy; it's a learned skill. You should learn it.

Don't make it about you. Business discussions are not about you. You don't have to be right and your customer wrong to convince them to buy your product or service. You want them to be right, and one of the things you want them to be right about is their upcoming decision to make a purchase from you. The discussion and the outcomes have to be about them.

One of our biggest clients engaged my company to provide some services that required a high level of expertise and experience. We had the perfect person—a guy named Ernie. The client wanted the work to be done in their offices due to concerns they had about data security. It was a perfectly legitimate concern, and we agreed to do this. Ernie worked in an office about forty miles away from the client's office. He did the drive for about two weeks and then complained to me that it was unnecessary and time-consuming. He thought the client's security concerns were overblown, and he hated making the drive. (I had a similar assignment early in my career, where I drove thirty-five miles each way for over seven years; I had very little empathy for Ernie.)

Ernie had a dualistic conception of this issue. He was positive that he was right and that the client was wrong. He asked me to talk with the client about letting him work remotely, which would entail access to their data through their firewall. I chatted with the client about this, and to no one's surprise, they said no. Ernie was upset and said he would no longer drive to the client's office. We found someone else to do the project. Ernie's inability to see the client's perspective was the inflection point here.

Client-focused people who break out of the dual world and live in the real world have developed a personal brand of curiosity, interest, and development. They are curious to know what their customer is thinking, what they really want or need, and what might be the specific factors that would influence their purchase decision. They want to know what makes a great experience for people, and they strive to deliver that. That's a real world that most people would value. That's an experiential brand that creates loyal clients. That's the reality of nonduality.

Let There Be Peace on Earth

And let it begin with me! You will not always find that clients are easy to deal with. Oftentimes, a client wants to interact with you because they are angry. Their discontent may have something to do with your product, your service, the service provided to them by someone else in your company, or perhaps the fact that their favorite English Premier League team just lost a match that they should have won. If they are angry and it's business related, you'll know. If they are angry for another reason and they are taking it out on you, that's definitely not fair or right, but it happens. You are the one who should be the peace giver.

The San Jose, California, airport is an updated, clean airport that has both domestic and international service. The vast majority of the flights in and out of San Jose are operated by Southwest Airlines. One day, I was sitting in the boarding area, waiting for my flight, when I saw an interesting and high-volume exchange between a very angry passenger and a Southwest gate agent. The exchange was about the passenger's access to a flight to a California destination. The passenger had arrived at the gate after the doors to the aircraft to his destination had closed, and he was telling the gate agent that his very strong desire was that she go down the jet bridge, knock on the door, and get them to reopen the door and allow him on to the flight.

You may wonder if I was eavesdropping. I can assure you that I was not and that the irate passenger's side of this entire conversation was being heard throughout the terminal. He was at full volume—his amp was turned up to eleven (as in *Spinal Tap*). Shouting, demanding, interrogating the gate agent, "Do you know I am?" I didn't know who he was, and my guess is that the gate agent didn't know him either, outside of the fact that he was a late, irate passenger who seemed to have forgotten how to treat another adult in a civil and respectful manner.

The gate agent got in a few words, and I guess I was eavesdropping on her response because she was neither loud nor belligerent. In fact, I thought her response could be characterized by the term *measured*. I might even call it kind. She never raised her voice. She didn't interrupt the irate passenger's lengthy tirades. She didn't react when he called her names or made irrational demands, because he clearly believed himself to be a very important person. She must have said, "I'm sorry, I can't do that, but I'd be happy to help you find an alternate flight to get you to your destination," at least ten times. That might be a low estimate, but she didn't waver.

It seemed like this went on for a very long time, but I'm sure it was no longer than a few minutes. I was stunned at the unabridged rudeness of the irate passenger and amazed at the aplomb and grace of the Southwest gate agent.

The irate passenger finally realized that he wasn't getting on that flight and stormed off. I ambled up to the gate and asked the gate agent if she would share with me what she was thinking during this exchange. She told me that this happens occasionally and that she has learned that the best thing she can do is to calmly offer an apology and suggest that she may be able to help the passenger get on a later flight.

Her goal is to deescalate the situation. She didn't cause it; the passenger caused it. For what is she apologizing? She's sorry that this person is in a bad spot. She's sorry that she can't get him on the plane. She's sorry that he is so distressed that he's yelling at her. She's sorry that he wasn't able to plan his time better. Maybe there was more traffic than he anticipated, or maybe the TSA screening line was longer than he thought it would be. Maybe he is trying to get to an important business meeting or family event. He's yelling, and she's sorry. That's peace giving.

She didn't know what happened with this passenger, and she didn't ask because the irate passenger wasn't about to get on that plane. Her job is to try and help him understand that and then rebook him on another flight. She told me that she likes helping people and will do whatever she can to help someone. She was trying to bring peace to the irate passenger. I hope he found it, and I hope he got to where he needed to go without disturbing another person's peace!

Look for Opportunities

Paying attention to someone means you have to look for opportunities to pay attention. David Maister, in his book *Strategy and the Fat Smoker*, says that creating a great experience for a client is often the result of many small gestures rather than one grand gesture. It is wise to look for opportunities to create a great experience in both of these categories. Let's explore them both.

Grand gestures can be beautiful things. Victor, who helped me with my car, was definitely in the grand gesture category. He saw an opportunity, and he delivered. He made a commitment to fix the problem by finding the spare part and sending a service technician to my home to install the part. He kept me informed of progress and made sure I was satisfied. That's a grand gesture. One big thing that makes your client say "**_WOW_**." Italics, caps, and underline are there just to emphasize this **_WOW_** from the common, everyday "wow."

The problem with a grand gesture is that it's a bit like cold fusion;

it's hard to replicate. Once you've helped your client in this amazing way, they may come to expect more grand gestures. They may even rely on you to fix things that they have messed up. They are, however, a great way to create a positive, memorable experience for a client.

On the other end of the spectrum of "creating experience" is the category of many small gestures. Your dentist does this for you, and you probably don't even realize it. They call you or text you to remind you of your appointment, they take care of billing your dental insurance for the services rendered, they let you know before they provide those services what your out-of-pocket costs will be, they make sure that their office is spotlessly clean, their reception staff are friendly and helpful, they let you know if an earlier appointment is available in case you may wish to get your teeth cleaned this week rather than wait until the end of the month, and many more. Why do they do this? They do it because they know they have to try to differentiate themselves from their competition. They look for opportunities to provide just a little bit extra in the hopes that you'll recognize that they are, in fact, providing you with something extra. They do this to keep you as a client because they know there are a lot of dentists out there who would like your business!

You may be a retail establishment or a window-cleaning service. How then could you do the many little things that cumulatively add up to service? This is where you look for opportunities to CARE for you client. Communicating with them in a timely manner, listening to their issues and concerns, delivering on time (or early if that's an option), and making sure that you understand their definition of excellence so that you can provide excellence to the client.

We had a client to whom I had personally committed that we would deliver intermediate work products on schedule or early. This included periodic meetings with the client to discuss our work. There were instances where our subject matter expert had a conflict and asked if we could move a meeting. My answer was no. We'll figure it out, and maybe the subject matter expert will have to join via a meeting app, but we don't mess with the schedule. We had a work product that was due to be delivered to the client on a Thursday in accordance with our schedule. We knew that this was the Thursday before a three-day weekend and that the client would not be in the office on Friday and obviously not on Monday. The team working on this asked me if we could delay the delivery until Tuesday so that they could do some extra work on the product. *No.* We don't mess with the schedule. The team then worked a bit extra to make sure that the product was excellent. It was delivered on time, and the client didn't even look at it until the following Thursday. I know that because they called me on that Thursday to apologize that they hadn't started to look at the work product yet *and* to thank me for getting it delivered on time.

It's the little things that count, and the ability to continue to do CARE-oriented things for your client is cumulative. It all adds up to a happy client who wants to do business with you over and over again.

We arranged to have the trees at our home trimmed using a service that we've used before. In our past experience, this service provider showed up on time, completed the job when he said he would, and did the work at what we felt was a reasonable price. All of these were little gestures that this service provider had done that got me to a spot where he was a preferred provider that I trusted.

The tree-trimming person met with me to discuss the scope of work—which trees I wanted him to trim and when would be an agreeable time to do the work. The service provider wanted to come on a Sunday. That was fine with me; I just mentioned that a neighbor had recently had a stump grinder clamoring away at his home on a Sunday afternoon, and I hoped that they would be quieter than the stump grinder. I think that tree trimming is, in general, quieter than a stump grinder; I was just chatting with the guy.

We agreed on a price, he showed up at the agreed-upon time, and I didn't hear any noise as he was working away in the trees. When he took a break, I asked him what he was doing that didn't generate tree-trimming noise, and he told me he decided to use a hand saw because he didn't want to disturb my Sunday afternoon, nor did he want to disturb the Sunday afternoons of my neighbors. He saw an opportunity and blew my mind.

One big opportunity bucket presents itself when something goes wrong. Memorable experiences, both good and bad, can be created by how the issue gets resolved. I had a dental problem—a crown that had recently been installed on one tooth chipped. It was the timing of this that was problematic, as it happened two days before one of my sons was getting married. I called the dentist, anxious about my smile. (I can say that the father of the groom is a mostly extraneous element of a wedding; no one was looking at me that day.) My dentist was on vacation but called me back within an hour. She had already made an appointment for me with another local dentist who temporarily fixed the issue. My dentist had one of her staff call me to set up an appointment for the following week to permanently fix the issue.

They took advantage of a "service recovery" issue to create a great experience. I was very appreciative that I was able to have a normal smile in the wedding photos even though, as I said, no one else would have noticed, nor would they have cared!

Pay attention to your clients. Do the little things on a consistent basis and take advantage of the opportunities to do the big things to create a positive, memorable experience for your client. The respect that you show them is cumulative; the more you do it, the more you build trust and loyalty.

Asked and Answered

The last thing here is one of my big personal peeves. Would you like to join our "frequent purchaser's club?" "Can I sign you up for our discount program?" "Wouldn't you like to have your phone number and email in our system to make future purchases easier?"

My answer is almost always no. I know many others who would have the same answer. Companies do this as a means of contact and collecting data. Many companies have policies, procedures, and scripted monologues for employees dealing with clients:

1. You have to ask the client at the point of sale if they "would like to …"

2. You can't take no for an answer.
3. When the client says no, you should have a rebuttal that explains why it is good for the client to sign up for the program.
4. When the client says no a second time, you should have a second rebuttal.
5. Drop it when the client threatens to leave!

It's fair to ask if someone wants to join your loyalty program. It's not fair to ask twice, much less three times.

In Costco, there is a line of Costco-related businesses on the way out of the store that often have one or two people trying to get you to upgrade your kitchen cabinets or put a solar power system on your home. The solar guy was there one day and through some Jedi mind trick got me to stop to talk with him even though I have solar panels on my roof. He was trying to talk me into additional panels and a couple of batteries. He asked one question relating to how much we actually paid for electricity in a year. When I answered, he looked me in the eye, smiled, and said, "You're good. You don't need this." One question, one answer. If there's interest, then keep going. Otherwise, let's all get on with our days. Well done, Costco solar power person!

R-Responsiveness

At its core, responsiveness means doing what you said you were going to do, when you said you were going to do it. It seems so simple.

"I'll be with you in two minutes."

"We can have your car ready by Thursday at noon."

"I'll have to check with the service department, and I'll call you tomorrow morning by ten to let you know the status of your request."

"We don't have that color in our inventory, but we can order it and have it for you in five business days."

"The doctor is out today, but she has arranged for one of her colleagues to see you and help you with your issue today."

All examples of responsiveness if the speaker does, indeed, follow through and get the product or provide the information or service in the stated time frame. All of us can think of a time when something was completed within the promised time, or a product we ordered was delivered late, or not delivered at all.

This is a lesson I learned the hard way. We had committed to deliver some technical documents to a client for their review by a certain date. I wasn't working on this project, but I knew the client and had been in the room when the commitment was made. Our team didn't deliver, and the client called me and lit me up. Deservedly so. We had made a commitment, and this client had blocked out time that day to review the documents. Our failure to deliver messed with her schedule.

It seems so easy—just do what you promise. Yet we all know how difficult that is because most promises made to clients do *not* solely depend on us. There's a team working on an engineering project, or warehouse and shipping employees who have to move something through the system to get it out to a client at the promised time. Maybe that's why so many promises are unkept. Perhaps this is also an opportunity for a company to find ways to get all employees on board with respect to keeping promises and being responsive.

The core of responsiveness is being on time. It's simply a temporal variable. I know something about this because I have been clinically diagnosed with extreme-punctuality-syndrome. I hate being late and tend to arrive early to most events. I remember my wife's grandfather telling me that he left for work twenty minutes earlier than he really needed to just in case he got a flat tire on the way to work and needed to change it. He also liked to be on time.

The extreme side of being on time was elucidated by the Hall of Fame football coach Vince Lombardi. He is reputed to have said, "If you are five minutes early, you are already ten minutes late." I think that's a bit too far, even for me. I like the rephrase of this quote that is often attributed to another Hall of Fame football coach, Bill Parcells, who said, "If you aren't five minutes early, you're late." That's a bit more reasonable.

There are those who are habitually late. I'll put these into three groups:

1. Inability to estimate how much time it takes to get something done
2. Just like to be late because that is who they are
3. Think it's a waste of time to be early and thus try to get their "exactly on time"

We'll talk more about bad estimating in the following section titled "Overconfidence." I don't think there is anything that I can say to the second or third groups, but, as you may suspect, I do have a story that is relevant to these groups.

My work colleague, who I'll call Roman, traveled quite frequently. I also traveled a lot. We were both on airplanes just about every week. One day, we were both on the same flight. I got to the airport early, got my upgrade to business class (I knew that Roman would also be upgraded), got on the plane with my appointed group, and got myself organized for a four-hour flight.

Roman was not on the plane when I boarded. As I sat there, I did not see him board the plane. The flight attendant advised all passengers to take their seats, as they were about to close the doors to the plane. I wondered if Roman had gotten sick, had a car accident, got called to another meeting in another city—I wondered if he was OK. A few seconds before the flight crew closed the doors, Roman slammed onto the plane with his bag and his briefcase. He was sweaty and breathing hard. I asked him if he was OK, and he said everything was fine, and I let it go.

When I got back to the office later that week, I asked Roman's assistant if she knew what happened to cause Roman to almost miss the flight. As it turns out, she knew exactly what happened. She told me that Roman proudly planned to get to every flight exactly fifteen minutes before the departure time. As an aside, that's really tough to do when you consider the variability of a security line at most major airports, including the airport that we flew from. She said he never told her if he missed a flight. She did know that he had come close to missing them from time to time.

On this particular evening, he had gotten to the security checkpoint and realized that he didn't have his ID; in fact, he didn't have his wallet. He got out of line, called his assistant, and asked her if his wallet was on his desk. She looked, and it wasn't there. Then he panicked and started screaming at her, asking her where he left his wallet. This particular assistant is a very nice person and is not a mind reader, so she told me that she got a little bit teary-eyed as she was being berated for not having sufficient omniscience to know where someone had left their wallet. Roman ran back to his car, hoping that he'd left his wallet there. He opened the car, and there, on the dashboard, was his wallet. He ran back to the security line, ran to the train, got off the train, ran to the gate, and just made it.

Roman thought it was a waste of time to be early, and he didn't mind being late. He did this with clients and coworkers. It's disrespectful and can cause you to elevate your heart rate to a dangerous level as you are sprinting to your plane. Do you want to live your life like that? I don't.

Overconfidence

An acquaintance was leaving his full-time job with a large publicly traded corporation and starting a consulting practice—a semiretirement move on his part. One of my colleagues thought that my acquaintance (I'll call him Sam) could be helpful, so he offered Sam a consulting contract, and it was the start of a beautiful relationship. I think Sam was very helpful to my colleague. I was happy to be able to help Sam out with a consulting gig, and I was happy that I could help out my colleague. Sam's corporate experience fit very nicely into the specific sector of the company for which my colleague was responsible.

Sam indicated to me that he would be able to help other sectors of my company. I asked what he thought he could do for these other sectors because, from my perspective, these other business sectors were way out of his swim lane. Sam confidently told me what he perceived was wrong with these business sectors and with the company as a whole. "Have you spoken to any other executives?" I asked him.

"No," he replied, "I didn't have to talk with anyone. I could just see what was wrong, and if I can get my contract expanded, I can help you." I told him I didn't think I could sell it, and the conversation ended there.

Overconfidence leads us to say and do things that we can't back up. I knew that Sam did not have any expertise in the areas where he claimed he could help us. Hiring him would have been a mistake for both of us.

Why is this part of responsiveness? It's part of responsiveness because this is where overconfidence and overpromising usually occurs. If you promise something you can't deliver, you can't be responsive. You can't meet your commitments.

A piece of technology that I had purchased was not working correctly, so I engaged the company's customer service department. I telephoned the service line and was told that this was a common problem that was solved by the installation of a new part. I was further told that I could expect a call within the next twenty-four to forty-eight hours to set up a time for a technician to come to my home and replace the part.

After waiting for forty-eight hours, I telephoned the service line a second time (around four o'clock in the afternoon) and spoke to a very nice person who told me that she would check with the service department the following day when they opened up because they were closed by then. (This service department was in my time zone, and the company's own recorded information told me that the service department was open from 6:00 a.m. to 7:00 p.m. in my time zone.) This very nice person told me that she would call me the next morning with any information she had. "That's terrific responsiveness," I said to myself.

The following day, I didn't get a call from the nice person, so I got back on the phone and waited forty-five minutes through a ninety-second loop of piano music to speak to another service rep. I really loved this nice person's confidence and commitment to service. She seemed like she would be the person who would finally help me—but sadly, that was not the case.

Finally, on my fifth try, I got through to someone on a Saturday morning who said that they could help and that I should expect a call first thing on Monday. I wasn't holding my breath, but to my surprise, I got the call on Monday morning, and the replacement part was installed by eleven o'clock that morning. The device has worked flawlessly since.

Everybody was really confident in their ability to get stuff done, yet one person out of the five I contacted was able to get me in the queue to get the part replaced. The Dunning-Krueger effect is the name given to a cognitive bias where people with limited ability in a specific area tend to overestimate their actual abilities. It was first described by Justin Kruger and David Dunning in 1999. I've been alive for a long time, and I have to wonder what took the psychology world so long to describe this bias that I've witnessed time and again since I was a young man.

This isn't about intelligence. It's simply that people often think they know more than they actually know or that they can do more than they can actually do. Researchers have seen the opposite for high-performing individuals. Many times, outstanding performers tend to underestimate their skills. For the non-high-performing world, we need to recognize that our confidence may push us to think we know more than we do, or to make commitments that we likely cannot keep.

We do this because, among other reasons, we like to think highly of ourselves. There's nothing wrong with that; we just need to inject a little reality into situations where we may be about to overcommit.

This can be boiled down to two specific elements: self-awareness and truth telling. I don't have to describe truthfulness, but the concept of self-awareness merits a few lines of text. People with high emotional intelligence are self-aware. They know what they can do, and they know what they can't do. They understand their strengths and their limitations. Emotional intelligence is about people skills and your ability to manage your emotions as well as successfully deal with the emotional responses of people around you.

Self-awareness is the element that helps you understand why you are feeling what you are feeling and thinking what you are thinking. It's often activated by asking yourself the simple question, "Why do I think or feel this way?" Overconfident people—those who are venturing into Dunning-Kruger territory—often are reacting in a way to please others, to be heroes, to be problem solvers, to be helpful. These aren't bad things necessarily, but your response moves into the unresponsive category when your overconfident response to your client cannot be backed up with your actions.

An angry client telephoned me at 1:00 p.m. and demanded that I meet with him that very afternoon. This was going to be brutal. It was a Friday, and I'd have to leave within fifteen minutes if I was to meet with him at the requested time, and it would take me around two hours to get home following the meeting. This is Los Angeles, and we don't measure driving in the form of miles; we measure it by time.

The client told me the problem, and I immediately committed to driving out to meet with him. If you think it sounds like this client wanted to punish me a little bit, you'd be right. He was very mad because the project manager who was handling his big pipeline replacement project had just lied to him about a technical issue that we were facing on the project. I don't recall exactly what our project manager told the client, and I don't recall the specific issue or even how the client knew that our person was not telling the truth. Simply put, they knew that someone had lied to them about a pretty important issue, and their unhappy meter was pegging.

Why did our person lie? Why didn't he just whip out his cell phone and call one of the numerous technical experts that we have in our company, all of whom also had cell phones? Surely he could have reached one of these experts and gotten the answer that was required. Perhaps no one was available. What then? Make a commitment to the client to get the answer and get back to him as soon as possible. "As soon as I can get in touch with one of our experts, I'll get you your answer, and I'll call you Monday first thing to give you a status update if I don't have an answer for you by that time." You might have responded differently. The main thing is to not let your overconfidence bait you into taking a guess at an answer that, if wrong, seems to be a lie. That's what my guy did. The client lost all confidence in this individual, I had to replace him on the project with another person, and we jointly had to work to rebuild the client's trust in us and our company.

Answer the Mail

Not much gets delivered into our mailboxes anymore. We get a few catalogues and maybe a bill that we haven't gotten around to setting up in paperless mode. Let's use the term *mail* to be a catchall for any type of communication outreach that a client might make to you. Simply get back to them quickly.

Most of us prefer to speak with someone about our issue, concern, or question while it is fresh in our mind. That's one of the best reasons to respond right away. If you don't know the answer, respond and tell them that you're working on getting the answer. And then get the answer for them.

Yelp is a source for finding a handyman. There are others, but I used Yelp. My regular handyman was not responding to my voicemail. I gave him forty-eight hours to respond, and I figured he was busy, so I queried Yelp, and I tried an experiment. I texted my regular guy, then called the next guy on the list and didn't leave a message, and then called the third guy on the list and left a message. That was at 11:00 a.m. on a Tuesday. At 11:15 a.m., the person that I called but didn't leave a message called me back. His name is Wes. He asked if I had called his number looking for a handyman (we all know that I was the one who did this), and after a brief discussion, I forwarded to him some photos of the problem for which I required his services, and he texted me back to see if Thursday at noon would be OK. It was; we had an appointment.

Later that night, my regular guy (I keep saying this—he's worked for me maybe three times in six years, which is also the sum total of my need for handyman-type services over this time frame) texted me and said he was tied up for three weeks. He's a really talented person, and

I'm happy that he's busy. I told him I needed it done sooner. Thursday morning arrives, and the third guy, who I'd called and left a message for on Tuesday, called and left a voicemail that he had received my voicemail and invited me to call him back. Ten minutes later, Wes showed up at exactly the time we had agreed upon and set about to fix the problem.

Perhaps this is simply a matter of volume. Maybe I'm overthinking this, and, in reality, the right way to go about this is to make a bunch of calls to service providers and just go with the one who gets back to you first or can get to you first to fix your problem. Is that a reality that any of us want to live in? Do you want to make six phone calls to people who have four Yelp reviews, trying to find someone who is available to solve your problem? Probably not. I want someone who responds in a reasonable amount of time to my query and then does what they say they are going to do by showing up on time and taking care of the issue for a reasonable price.

Wes was very reasonable and very professional. I needed to replace a bathroom fan that had failed and, after purchasing the identically sized model as a replacement, couldn't figure out how to get the old one out. It looked to me like I'd have to cut dry wall, install the new fan, repair and repaint the dry wall, and pray that the color of the paint matched the existing one.

Wes listened to me and simply asked if there was a way to get into the attic. There was. He had a better way to fix this problem. He did it from above rather than from below. If you are good at home repairs, you may be saying, "Duh—everyone knows that." You're wrong because I didn't know that, but Wes did. So here was a service provider who was responsive, paid attention to me, offered a better way to make the repair, and did excellent work at a fair price.

Everything has to come together for Wes to be successful. He has to be responsive. He has to pay attention to his clients to make sure he fully understands their needs. Finally, he has to deliver excellence. Since I didn't know how to replace the fan, I think a fair question you could ask is, "How did I know he did excellent work?" That is an excellent question. I don't. What I do know is that he was very careful to not damage floors or other fixtures in the bathroom. He thoroughly cleaned up his working area, including wiping off his dirty palm prints from the attic access door. And the fan worked like a champ—about twenty times in a row as I giddily switched it on and off. It's the attention to the little things that give me rise to believe that the work was done well.

That's great, but doesn't everyone know that you've got to do all of these things in a competitive service field? Yes, they do, but I challenge you right now to go to Yelp, pick out three handyman service providers to call, call them, and see if they get back to you. You'll quickly find out who can answer the mail.

Time after Time

We are busy people, and our time is valuable. Our calendars are filled with appointments, phone calls, Zoom calls, meetings, and lunch dates. We run from call to call, from meeting to meeting. We strive to be on time, and we don't like it when we delay our lunch so that we can show up on time for a noon meeting, while a couple of our colleagues show up ten minutes late because they took the time to have lunch. When I say "we," I really mean "me."

I'm a punctual person, and that's a blessing and a curse. I don't like to be late for meetings, Zoom calls, or lunch dates because I don't want people to be forced to wait for me. This could be a genetic flaw or some type of neurosis; I just know that it exists for me. As a result, I decided to research punctuality so I could write about it, thinking I might be able to sway a few of the folks who are habitually nonpunctual over to my side of the field.

There must be more to the concept of punctuality than a bimodal formulation of "on time is good" and "not on time is bad." It's way more complicated than this. In fact, it's so complex that there's little conclusive research into the subject of punctuality, and the research that does exist is generally contradictory. Each of us knows people who live to be on time (again, full disclosure, I'm in that tribe) and those who have a much more fluid concept of punctuality. We can learn from ourselves and our colleagues, and we can learn a bit from whatever research is out there on this topic. We're going to examine punctuality from two perspectives: what in someone's brain or DNA causes them to be punctual and how punctuality (or the lack thereof) can be driven by culture.

Is Punctuality Genetic or a Learned Behavior?

The answer is probably both. One psychologist prepared a report on a number of patients who were habitually late. They didn't intend to be late, but there was always something, often described as a trauma or neurosis, that led them to this behavior. An example might be that they had a parent who was always late and felt that being on time was a waste of time because lots of other people were late. For others (and I can relate to this), there was a parent or authority figure who was always on time, and punctuality was drilled into them. In the days when phones had rotary dials, I can recall my father yelling at me to return a phone call because he had told my friend that I would call him back by 6:00 p.m.—and thus I had to meet the time commitment dumped on me by my father.

Some not-on-timers like the thrill of trying to get there just in time. Like my colleague Roman who felt that arriving any earlier than fifteen minutes before the flight departure time was simply a waste of time. You want to know what else is a waste of time? Sitting in the airport for three hours because you missed your flight. You can't control all of the variables that exist within the airport system of parking your car, going through security, and getting on the tram. I know that Roman periodically missed flights and was often late to meetings, but it seems that he did get his adrenaline fix.

The punctual people have their own suite of neuroses and traumas. This is well beyond the remit of this book. It is safe to say that punctual people get things done on time and probably need therapy as much, or more, than the nonpunctual people of this world.

There is one more punctuality factor worth noting—culture. A

German soccer player named Miroslav Klose, who played for several years on an Italian club team, experienced this cultural dyslexion. Herr Klose, who was a star of the German national team, said that, in Italy, he had to learn to let up on some German things that he was used to, like accuracy and punctuality.

Another aspect of punctuality is getting stuff done on time. That's really at the core of responsiveness. Do you do what you said you were going to do, when you said you were going to do it? Most of the professors that I had in college wouldn't let someone turn in an assignment after the due date. I recall one particular assignment in graduate school that required the completion of a four-page analysis of a specific water treatment process. Four typed pages due on a date certain. One of my classmates wrote nine pages and turned in the assignment three weeks late. He reasoned that he had prepared a superior paper and that the superiority of his thinking outweighed his inability to comply with both the four-page requirement and the time requirement.

Lost time is something that one can never get back. When you make a time commitment to a customer to deliver a product or service, you need to keep that commitment. Did my convenience store experience have a time commitment? No, it did not. The convenience store in my first example has no explicit or implicit commitment to timeliness. Their only commitment is to convenience, however that may be defined. Would a quick response by the person working at the store have changed my day? No. It could only have saved me a minute or two, and in reality, that wasn't going to change my world or my life in any appreciable way. But if timeliness and responsiveness in that convenience store could make a difference for someone else and could be a differentiator for that store, then maybe they should start thinking about how to create a bit of a positive experience.

Asymmetric punctuality is a concept that you may not have heard about, but you have definitely experienced it. You show up on time for an appointment with your doctor, and you end up having to wait some chunk of time past the appointed hour to see the doctor. You show up on time for a flight, and then you have to wait because the incoming flight is late or there is a mechanical issue they need to fix. I recently suffered through jury duty and experienced asymmetric punctuality on steroids. I was told to report to a courtroom at 2:30 p.m. They lined us up to go into the courtroom at 3:30 p.m., and then we stood in line for another fifteen minutes before they ushered us into the courtroom. We then waited five more minutes for the judge to enter, who then took another ten minutes to explain why he was late. Then he dismissed us for the day.

My doctor's medical group sent me a survey following a visit to their urgent care facility. On this particular visit, I saw a very kind and effective nurse practitioner who listened to me, did some analysis, and gave me a prescription that solved the issue. The medical group asked if I would fill out a survey with respect to this visit, which I did because I thought the nurse practitioner was great. The survey asked a bit about people, like receptionists and nurses and others. The first question is the one that surprised me. "Did we see you within fifteen minutes of your appointment?" In this case, they had.

The larger question, though, is why are they giving themselves a fifteen-minute cushion? Almost no other service business does this. I realize that in medicine, there are issues that arise with patients that take a medical professional out of their prearranged schedule. That shouldn't really be the case in an urgent care clinic because if there was something that required more attention, it would likely be rendered by specialists, not the emergency room doctors and nurse practitioners. In reality, it doesn't matter to me, as I go to this medical group because they take my insurance and I like my primary care physician. I'd be a lot happier if they were always punctual, but this may be the singular profession for which most of us will cut some slack on not being punctual.

If you make time commitments, you should live by those time commitments. I realize that there are many factors impacting a doctor's schedule, and if she's running late, it's because someone needed her time more than I did. When a person in a retail shop says, "I'll be right with you" and then proceeds to not be right with me, it might not be their fault. They could be working with a client who takes a bit of extra time or has some other issue that they need to resolve. My advice is simply this: set realistic time expectations for your clients and strive to meet those.

Availability

Another great piece of advice from Bill Parcells, who once said, "The greatest ability is availability." This was said about American football, a violent sport where players get injured and are thus unavailable to play. His premise was that players who could avoid injury could be available to play.

You likely don't worry about injuries to someone engaged in sales or client account management. What you do want is people who are available when a client needs them. That is probably less of a problem in a retail organization. Staff are engaged to work specific shifts, and some are assigned to be available to engage with clients should they have a question about merchandise. While that sounds simple, many managers of retail stores can tell you about sales associates who take long smoke breaks in the alley behind the store or hide out in a bathroom or breakroom just to avoid working.

In an age of remote working, availability is a different story for services organizations. I recently got an email from a client at about 5:45 p.m. asking me if we could reschedule a meeting that was set to occur the following day. I was about to teach a class and knew I wouldn't be home until maybe 10:00 p.m. All I had was my phone, and I wanted to check calendars for multiple people to see when the best time would be to reschedule the meeting. I simply told her that I would reschedule things when I got home that night and that she would see the new meeting notice the following morning, and that's what I did.

You can't always do something right away. If you can, then do it. If you can't, then advise your client of the time when you'll take care of things and make sure you do what you said you were going to do.

Trust Me, You'll Love It!

A local business offers art training classes for all ages, with a focus on children. Kids like to draw, paint, and sculpt. I think a ten-year-old would love to have someone give them a mess of steel and iron scrap and a blow torch so they could make art.

Potential clients often engage this business first by telephone. They call to understand the training programs, costs, schedule, and so on. The business has marketing specialists who are trained to take these calls and provide information about their services. The marketing specialist is required to give the prospective client a long speech, regardless of what the client is asking about.

Here are some typical questions. "Do you sell art supplies?" "What types of adult classes do you have, and what do they cost?" "Can you teach a one-year-old to paint?" These are all answered with the long speech that focuses on training for kids.

Within that speech is the answer to the question about teaching a one-year-old, but it doesn't address the other questions. It's not responsive. The specialists aren't allowed to use their skills and training to help potential customers. Rather, they are using something that someone in the company's marketing department wrote and thinks is a killer speech.

Canned presentations, speeches, or giant bunches of words that are not on point and are taken too far are perceived by your potential client as a farce. It's almost always a negative experience that has limited upside and lots of downside with respect to attracting new business.

Answer people's questions. Give them the information they seek. Be accurate. Be brief. Be focused. Then, if you still have their attention, and only then, you might be able to give them the chief marketing officer's screed.

E-Excellence

Doing excellent work, providing excellent service, and delivering excellent products—these are very difficult things to do. The reason for that is we, as the service provider or the producer/retailer of a product, do not define excellence. The client does that. If you don't communicate *and* pay attention to your client, you'll have a very low chance of providing excellence to them. You can get lucky, but I think I'd rather be really good at being excellent.

Our client was a water department of a city on the West Coast of the US. They were a long-term client, and the client service manager, project manager, and technical service provider for this client was a really smart guy named Aaron. As those titles imply, Aaron did everything for this client, and he had just completed the preparation of a study that was leading to the design of some mechanical upgrades and fixes for one of this client's facilities. Aaron told me that we were a slam dunk to compete for and win the next phase of the work, where an engineering firm would prepare the detailed design of these upgrades.

We prepared a proposal and were asked to participate in an interview with the client to talk about our proposal and how we would execute these upgrades. Two other firms were also competing for the work, and our team was quite sure we would be awarded the project. To our surprise, we were not awarded the project. The city gave the work to another company that had zero experience working with this particular city. Even more surprising is that we were ranked third out of the three firms that competed for the work. We came in dead last.

We asked the client if they would give us some feedback on our proposal, and we set up a virtual meeting with the client. I attended this meeting and asked Aaron to *not* attend the meeting. My thinking was that Aaron might be part of the problem, but I just wasn't sure, and I wanted the client to feel comfortable telling us if, indeed, this was the case.

The meeting started with the client telling us how much they liked Aaron. I believed this, as he is a very smart, likeable person. They told us that they selected the other firm because they thought that they had more experience with mechanical rehab engineering projects. "Have you ever worked with them before? Had you ever heard of them prior to them submitting a proposal?" I asked. "Nope" was the answer. That's a bit concerning because in a mature market like environmental engineering, it's extraordinarily rare that a public agency will select an engineering firm that they don't know to do work for them. I was stunned, particularly as the client continued to sing Aaron's praises.

Toward the end of our allotted one-hour meeting, I decided to be blunt and ask them specifically if there was anything that we had done that had been problematic for them. "Well, yeah," one of the client people sheepishly replied. He went on to tell me that, in the work we had just completed for them, they had three major problems. The first was that they thought we were too expensive because we had not been able to complete the work within the original budget and had requested a contract amendment for additional funds to complete the project. The second was that we had included some information in the report that they had explicitly asked us to not include. The third was that we refused to provide some information in the report that they had specifically asked us to include.

There were reasons for all of these, and I think Aaron, as the project manager, probably did what he thought best to meet the client's needs, despite their clear directions. Aaron was very sure that we had provided an excellent engineering work product to this client. What Aaron thought was irrelevant because the client thought differently. As much as they liked Aaron, they didn't get excellence from him and his team. They were unhappy.

The interesting thing is that clients often won't tell you that they are unhappy, especially if they like the people who are providing the service. It took this client fifty-five minutes and me asking them specifically where we had messed up for them to tell us that, in fact, we had not delivered excellence, as they defined it, to them and therefore would not be doing the next, and much more lucrative, phase of the work. That's a problem that we should have known about and fixed much earlier on—and we're going to give some thoughts on how to do that.

Excellence Is in the Eye of the Beholder

We don't define excellence. As we just discussed, our clients define excellence. One way we can better understand what a client might be looking for is to periodically check in with them. The following discussion is aimed at service providers, but retailers can figure out how to adapt this to their situations.

There's an app that you can put on your smartphone called "Map My Run." This app can be adjusted to provide performance feedback at variable intervals during your activity. When I first used the app, I got feedback at five-mile intervals. This was problematic since I was only going about five miles; I was getting feedback at the end of my run. I adjusted the app to give me feedback at one-mile intervals, and my times immediately improved (basically, I went from painfully slow to really slow). I also found that if my mind wandered during my run and I started to slow down, the feedback at the mile interval provided me information that encouraged me to start to run faster. When I run, I get objective feedback *early and often*, and I use that to adjust my performance to meet my expectations.

We strive to deliver products and services that meet or exceed our clients' expectations, and we often ask our clients at the end of the transaction if we have met or exceeded their expectations. Quite often, we use surveys or other impersonal means to gather this information. And that's the problem. We ask the client for performance feedback *at the end*. Are we then surprised at the client's negative feedback?

My company provided engineering and construction services. These projects have durations that range from months to years. If you are engaged in services or a transaction with a client that has a longer time frame, here are some ideas for getting useful feedback from your clients.

1. Get feedback without asking for it. Find a time that is convenient for your client to talk with them about the project on a routine basis. Talk about the work that you have completed, the work you are planning to complete in the next period of time (week, month, quarter, etc.), and any ongoing issues you are facing, along with your plan to address those issues. Be sure to create some space in your discussion to allow the client to respond to what you are saying, and make sure that you listen carefully to what they are telling you.

2. Be prepared to hear bad news and be prepared to act on it quickly. We want our clients to tell us when there are problems so that we

can fix them quickly and efficiently. As a general rule, the longer the problem lingers, the more expensive it is to correct. Sometimes there are problems with the quality of our work. Sometimes we have problems with schedule and are late in delivering work products. When you have a strong relationship with your client, you can directly ask about quality and schedule, and you can expect them to give you direct feedback. This will only happen when there exists a trust relationship between two individuals *and* when the individual receiving the feedback acts on it. When you fail to act on the feedback you receive from your client, you lose trust. In most cases, you will likely not get any additional feedback from that client because it's hard for most people to continuously give negative feedback. Find the problem and fix it fast.

3. Give the client feedback on *their* feedback. Let your client know how you are making adjustments in light of their feedback and then provide them with objective information about how your work quality is improving or how you have worked to get back on schedule. Feedback provides a great opportunity for you to spend time with your client in both getting information and responding to the information that the client provides.

4. Always get feedback at the end of a project. In addition to getting the feedback "every mile," get feedback when you finish your "run." Use some type of formal process that gives you actionable data.

Clients want to do business with organizations they trust. Getting frequent feedback and acting on that feedback is a great way to build trust with your client.

Comparative Excellence

Very few people can talk about an excellent product or service in and of itself. For most people, they are looking at excellence in a comparative fashion. If someone tells you that the clothing they just purchased is of the highest quality, they must, by definition, be comparing it to other clothing that is lower quality.

Prospective clients constantly compare. Every new electric vehicle is compared to Tesla. Watches, breakfast cereals, toaster ovens, legal services, knives, athletic shoes, and just about every other item on this planet exists in a competitive space. Manufacturers, retailers, and service providers need to think about their excellence in terms of the specific value provided by their product or service and how the product or service is different and better than a competitive offering.

Better is a well-known term. It's great to say that you have a better product or provide better service. In reality, your product or service is not better unless your client declares it to be better. And simply being better isn't sufficient for long-term success. You have to have a *differentiated* better. The service or product you are offering must be better in a way that is different from your competition. Absent this, many potential clients will go to your competitors because they will not believe that you are simply better. I think this is a well-understood concept.

Here's where the problem comes in. We often make "better" claims for our products or services by offering the client our comparison. This hit me while listening to an excellent podcast called *Pivot* hosted by a journalist named Kara Swisher and a marketing professor at New York University Stern School of Business named Scott Galloway. It seemed like a throwaway line, but it might not have been one. Scott Galloway called the city of Chicago the "Old Navy" of cities; you get 80 percent of New York City at 50 percent of the price. Old Navy is the low-priced offering of the series of stores owned by the Gap. I thought it was funny and insightful, and even though I wrote it down as soon as I could (I was driving when I heard this), I may have the percentages a bit off.

This was likely intended as a compliment to the city of Chicago. I've worked in both New York City and Chicago, and they are both fantastic places to visit, with lots of great restaurants and many things to do. New York has Broadway, the Empire State Building, Central Park, phenomenal art museums like MOMA, the Guggenheim, and the Whitney, and lots of tourist attractions. Chicago has great comedy clubs and theaters, Lake Erie, wonderful restaurants, and the Bean. Both are great cities; maybe Scott was right. It's up to you to decide—and that's the problem. How do you really know?

This made me think a bit more about comparisons. Often, we'll say that our product is just like some other higher-priced product or that our service is just as good as some other better-known service provider. Are those fair comparisons?

In light of Scott Galloway's comment on Chicago, I'm wondering if telling someone that you are offering them an Old Navy–type product, 80 percent of the quality and 50 percent of the price, actually makes sense. Perhaps it's not the wisest approach for sales and client interaction.

I recently visited a car dealer to look at a vehicle that had just been named Car of the Year by a national automotive magazine. I was curious to see this vehicle after reading the glowing review. It was indeed a beautiful car. The showroom had exactly one of these cars—red exterior with gray wheels that perfectly complemented the exterior paint color. This was coupled with a black and red interior that could have been stitched together in an Italian custom furniture shop. Stunning.

The salesman came over, introduced himself, and immediately started talking about the car. He said that the car company had gone out and poached top designers from other luxury car manufacturers. "Doesn't the front end remind you of a Bentley?" he asked. It definitely looked like a Bentley Continental GT grill. He commented that the back end of the car looked like a Porsche SUV and then told us that designers from both of these companies had been hired to help design and build this beautiful vehicle.

This led me to this specific question: "Do you want something that looks like an excellent product, or do you want the excellent product itself?" I don't want a car that looks like a high-end luxury car. I want a car that has a distinctive look that I like. Frankly, it doesn't even have to be all that great looking if it has the features I want. I do know that the next time a salesperson tells me that the product is just like some other high-end product, my next move will be to go and look at the real thing, not the wannabe. It's great to be aspirational, but I'll question a product or service that is aspiring to be excellent and look for products and services that are, indeed, excellent.

Getting It Right Is the Right Thing

We all want to do the right thing for our clients. The question is, what does the client think is the right thing? The answer is that many times, clients don't even know what's right. We can sort through this a bit.

The right thing starts with what the client thinks is right, if they are even able to articulate this. "The customer is always right" is an old business saying. It's not really true. Sometimes the customer makes a demand or asks you to do something that your company doesn't do. Sometimes they ask you to do something that might border on the ethical or legal lines in which your business operates. There are times when the customer is not right, but that's not what I want to talk about. When I had a customer ask me to do something that was unethical, I said, "No." That customer fired us and moved on to another firm that had softer ethical boundaries.

This is about making sure the customer gets what they need and, if possible, what they want. The best example I can think of is taken from the 1947 movie *Miracle on 34th Street*. In this movie, there is a character who believes that he is the real Santa Claus. He gets a job playing Santa Claus at Christmastime in the flagship Macy's Department Store in Manhattan. Santa asks each child who visits him at Macy's what they would like for Christmas, and the children happily oblige by telling Santa exactly what they want. One little boy asks for a specific brand of toy truck. Santa tells the boy that he can count on getting that for Christmas, and then he turns to the little boy's mother and tells her that this specific brand of truck is not available at Macy's. He lets her know that she can get this toy truck at Gimbel's Department Store, which is Macy's top rival in New York City.

Macy's could not help this boy's mother fulfill his Christmas wish.

Santa Claus, however, made it right. He directed her to the store where she could procure the toy truck that her child wanted. The problem here is that he worked for Macy's, and his recommendation for the mother to go to Gimbel's set off a firestorm within Macy's. While Mr. Macy is very upset with Santa, he comes to learn that the sales volume at Macy's has actually increased in light of Santa's willingness to help the customer solve their problem.

You don't always have to direct someone to another store to make it right for them. There are other ways to do this.

Andrew works for an educational technology company (let's call this company *School*) as an account executive. His job is not selling; rather it is making sure that the clients, which are school districts, have the software components they need and are able to use his company's software effectively and efficiently.

One of his clients had engaged a small company to provide an important software component that linked with the software that *School* provided. This small company had never done anything on this scale before and was struggling to build the software package that could integrate with *School's* software. Andrew jumped in and asked *School's* software engineers to help this client by helping the small company overcome some of the issues they were facing. The small company was finally able to deliver the software product that they were contracted to provide.

This is an example of creating a memorable experience for your client by simply doing the right thing. *School* got no money, no additional sales, and no contract extensions, but they did get one big thing out of this. The client recognized that *School* had invested some of their own time and expertise to make things right. They weren't making their product right; they were making another company's product right. That's what I mean by doing the right thing is the right thing to do.

Nordstrom is known for service. I went in one afternoon to purchase a very specific type of shirt. Nordstrom had several options, and a salesperson offered to help me. I tried on two of the options that were produced by different European fashion houses, and neither fit right. I explained this to the salesperson, and she directed me to another brand that she said she was confident would fit me correctly. She was right, and I went to purchase the shirt. She started to fold the shirt and then looked at me and said, "Not this shirt." I was a bit stunned, and she could see the look of confusion on my face. She explained to me that she thought the shirt I had brought up to her to purchase was returned merchandise. Someone had purchased that particular garment and returned it to the store. "How can you tell?" I asked her. "I just can," she said, "and I'm not letting you purchase this." She helped me find another that was in my size that had not been previously purchased.

There was nothing wrong, in my opinion, with the returned merchandise. I would never have known that it had been purchased and returned. There was something wrong with it in the opinion of the salesperson, who made it right by not allowing me to purchase it. In her mind, it was the right thing to do.

Choose Your Next Words Carefully

We use words to describe our company, our products, and our services. Many times, these words are superlatives. These are terms like "world-class," "best in class," "handpicked," "best quality," and many others. They are not to be confused with comparative words such as "faster," "better," or "cheaper" even though these words can also be misused and overused. Let's get back to superlatives and why they don't work.

One of the reasons superlatives don't work is that they are simply overused. In the 2003 movie *Elf,* Will Ferrell's character, Buddy the Elf, sees a sign on the door of a New York City coffee shop and walks in, yelling, "Congratulations!" and then walks out. The sign says, "World's best coffee." "Best" is used so much it has essentially lost its meaning in a marketing or sales context. My question is, "Who says it's the best?"

Coffee isn't the only product that organizations like to declare *best*.

In the southern end of Orange County, California, where I live, I've seen the following signs:

- world's best-made sandals
- world-class margaritas (at a steak house, not a Mexican restaurant)
- world's finest chocolates
- world's best surfboards

It's possible that some of these claims are true (I'm pretty sure the best margarita claim isn't true, but I could be wrong). These are self-proclaimed triumphs. The International Steak House Margarita Association isn't touring the world, ranking margaritas in steak houses. These are claims that, when one stops to think about it, are meaningless. It is possible that, because of my marketing background, I'm particularly sensitive to these words and claims. When I hear "best" or 'world-class," I simply discount it has highly unlikely or puffery. That's the right word because *Merriam-Webster* defines puffery as "exaggerated commendation especially for promotional purposes."

This is not the right way to communicate the attributes of a product or service with a potential client. The right way is to simply communicate the attributes. In the engineering world, we like to tell clients that we are "best in class" or that we offer them a "handpicked" team. The first superlative belies the fact that the engineers working for our competitors were all educated at the same universities, have similar levels of experience, and, in some cases, actually once worked for my company, where they were described as "best in class."

As to the latter claim, I'm wondering what it means with respect to proposing a team of engineers to work on a project. Does this mean that we offer lesser teams to other clients? Does it imply that we carefully inspect each engineer to make sure they are disease-free before we nominate them to serve on the project team? It's a term that makes sense for fruit but doesn't make sense for people. It sounds good. It sounds like something special, but it's mostly a hollow claim that just doesn't have significant meaning.

Know your products and services. Offer the positive attributes of your products and services that best meet your clients' needs. Try to stay away from meaningless superlatives and other types of word salad that don't really express the true value your product or service may bring to your client.

Impress Me

Experience is often some combination of quality, cost, time, and client impressions. Impressions are one of the major aspects of experience that can be controlled by the client interface—the person interacting with the client. It is these impressions that often are the difference between a client feeling that their interaction with the business was excellent or it was not. It seems that this may be a bimodal outcome.

Savile Row, in London, is home to many iconic tailor and menswear shops. My family was on vacation in London, and I went into Gieves and Hawkes at 1 Savile Row in London with my wife and four children. Obviously, I was a tourist. I wanted to buy a shirt from the former uniform maker for the Duke of Wellington, King George III, and pop star Michael Jackson (he wore a custom-made tailcoat during his *Bad* tour in the late 1980s). The building at 1 Savile Row was built by the Fairfax family in 1732. Gieves and Hawkes were founded in 1771. I had done my research, and I was ready to buy something that I could afford—like a shirt. Price and time weren't at issue. Quality was a given. I simply wanted to buy a little piece of English history, knowing full well that one shirt would be expensive.

A salesman approached me and asked if he could help me. I told him I was interested in shirts and gave him my size. He disdainfully directed me to a wall that had shirts in that size and then promptly left me alone. I selected a shirt and then tried to find out how to purchase it. Finally, a different staff member had pity on me after about ten minutes of wandering around and helped me purchase the shirt. My guess is that they tired of my large American family wandering around their store and wanted me out of there.

The initial salesperson clearly wanted nothing to do with me and did nothing at all to impress me with respect to service or to even say anything to me about quality, value for money, or the iconic history of Gieves and Hawkes. Perhaps he was hoping that I was going to purchase a bespoke (that's the English term for custom) suit. Maybe he didn't like Americans tourists. He may have noticed my family with me and immediately knew that I wasn't worth his time. Whatever his reasoning, the experience was lousy, but the shirt was fine, if a bit overpriced and pretentious for a midlevel executive in an engineering consulting practice.

As a sidenote, the term *impression* has not always had a positive meaning in England. The British Royal Navy, between 1664 and the early nineteenth century, used to *impress* men into service aboard their ships. This was essentially forced conscription into naval service, although they limited their target market to men between the ages of eighteen and fifty-five who might be capable of surviving life on an English warship. Here, we are talking about *impress* as a positive term— as in to leave someone with a positive impression or good feeling about a business.

The experience of going into Gieves and Hawkes was, for me, very interesting. A historically important shop that tailored clothes for some massive historical figures. I didn't even mind the "American with a family treatment" I got. I did wonder if this salesperson could turn on the charm for an English titan of industry and turn off the charm for an American tourist.

This is the key point. Most people can't turn it on and turn it off. Actors can do this, of course. Sociopaths as well! For most of us, the ability to make a strong, positive, excellent impression on a client has to be a part of who we are. This is not natural for many people and takes some practice and mentoring. Even though I had purchased an excellent shirt and had visited an iconic English men's shop on Savile Row, the "oh, it's just another American tourist" treatment that I received left me feeling less than excellent. That was my impression. I wasn't impressed.

Accurate Is Excellent

Engaging a client in a discussion of a product or service often involves a discussion regarding some specific aspect, or aspects, of the product or service. These are often performance related: this car has a fuel efficiency of thirty miles per gallon; this shirt should last you three years with normal use; your Lasik surgery to correct your vision should last fifteen years; these shoes are waterproof. You can think about lots of other product and service claims that you have heard when making a purchase decision.

The problem is that many salespeople are prone to exaggerate. Honestly, sometimes they aren't making up the exaggeration; they are just repeating what their company has told them or information from product literature they have been given. One excellent way to deliver excellence in service to your client is to be accurate. This means understanding the service and technical parameters to a level that enables you to provide accurate information to a client or to quickly access such information if you don't have it at your fingertips. I earlier talked about the residential solar power salesperson who told me he didn't have the information I was seeking but would get it for me in a certain period of time, which he did to my satisfaction.

Sometimes, however, a salesperson will just make something up to overcome an objection by a client or provide information to the client. I was at the Audi dealer waiting for my car to be "brought down" to me from the service department. Audi had just introduced their new electric vehicle, which they called an E-tron, and they had one on the lot. I was staring at it. It's a nice-looking car, and I was just starting to investigate electric vehicles.

A salesperson saw me looking—no, staring—at the car and jauntily walked over to me saying, "I can tell you love it. Let's go for a test-drive." I politely declined, explaining that they were bringing my car down from service and it should be down any minute. "Come on, man," he said. "It'll be at least another fifteen minutes, and there's no big deal if it sits there waiting for you. Let's drive this thing."

He was right about the timing of the car being delivered to me from the service department, so I agreed to do a test-drive. I really liked the car, but I explained that my biggest objection (besides the very high price) was the reported range of two hundred miles. Without hesitation, the salesman said that the EPA-reported ranges are assessed with a fully loaded car—four or five adults plus luggage. "This thing will easily do 280 miles in range," he overconfidently asserted. That didn't seem right to me, and we now know that most EVs will not go the full EPA range *and* that most EV manufacturers recommend charging the battery to only 80 percent of maximum to extend the battery life (which also serves to limit the range). I didn't buy the car. I didn't even consider Audi when evaluating EVs to purchase. Accuracy is excellence.

Excellence and Trust

Excellence is a promise that is understood by your clients to be continuous. Once you promise and deliver excellence, you are committed to delivering excellence. As long as you do so, your clients will trust that you will deliver excellence. They may even allow you to value price your product or service—that is, you may be able to charge more because you deliver excellence, and you can be trusted to continue to deliver excellence.

My company was not the most expensive, but we were definitely not a low-cost provider. We provided engineering and construction services, and the prices of our services varied but not by much. My goal, with the clients served by my group, was to reach the excellence and trust quadrant; I wanted clients to trust that they would get excellence every time they procured our services. If they wanted to buy low-cost services, that was their prerogative. Excellence and a great experience were what we wanted to offer our clients.

Pricing doesn't necessarily have to fit into this discussion, but you can't have expensive without it being excellent. You can have excellence without it being expensive. You can price your product or service wherever you like, but if you are expensive (or more expensive than your competition), you had better be excellent.

This concept applies to products as well. Many products are positioned as luxury or high-end goods that command a higher price due to their quality and/or value. Often there are specific assertions made about these products that may have to do with their market position (e.g., one of a kind, or handmade) or may be an assertion about the products themselves (low maintenance, made of tungsten carbide, etc.).

The CEO of my company got me started with a British shirtmaker (with a shop on Jermyn Street where all the old shirtmakers had shops). They have an online presence, and I liked being able to purchase shirts from their store. I don't like to iron shirts, so I preferred the noniron variety of shirt fabric because (and I believe this is self-explanatory, but I'll explain it anyway) I don't like to iron. What I've noticed, however, is that while some of the fairly expensive noniron shirts from this company look fantastic after being laundered, there are others that come out of the clothes dryer looking like they have been rescued from the bottom of the clothes hamper after a six-month exile from the clothes closet.

If the product says noniron, shouldn't all the shirts be noniron, and shouldn't they all come out of the dryer looking like they don't require ironing? I found this very troubling, and after more than twenty years of almost exclusively buying shirts from this one company, I switched to two other companies, both of which offer noniron shirts that all look fantastic after every washing/drying cycle. They are excellent shirts. Most of the shirts I bought from the British company were also excellent. It only took two shirts to turn me off. Accuracy is excellence, and that accurate excellence has to be delivered nearly 100 percent of the time to keep a client from switching—because excellence must engender trust.

CARE

Communication, *attention*, *responsiveness*, and *excellence* are the key words in the framework I developed to try to create a positive, memorable experience for our clients. These words were used to create an acronym that people could remember, one that would help guide them in their dealings with clients. We wanted to be the company that did great work that met our clients' needs, *and* we wanted our clients to have a great experience working with our company.

You may need a different acronym for your company. You may want to focus on other aspects of client experience that you believe will create a great experience for your clients. CARE, per se, doesn't necessarily work for every business or organization. It's a big, bad world out there, with many different types of retail and service businesses and many different types of organizations. Find what works for your clients and develop it so that your employees have some guidelines, framework, and examples for their client interactions.

The best companies understand what their clients consider to be a great experience and have their own framework, acronym, or guidelines for creating that experience. I think you'll find that whatever you develop for your company, there will be aspects of communication, attention, responsiveness, and excellence that will be meaningful to your clients. It's about their experience in dealing with you, and you have the ability to manage that thoughtfully and CAREfully.

CHAPTER THREE

Getting Everyone on Board

Big organizations that desire to make exceptional experience part of their brand recognize that such service is provided by their people. This is not only the people who interact with clients. If a company truly implements CARE, everyone has to deliver. The people in the factory making the product have to ensure they make excellent products and that those products are produced in a timely, efficient manner. The billing department needs to make sure they get their bills out to the clients at an appropriate time and that they are accurate. And the list goes on.

Everyone has to be on the bus. Everyone has to be on board with the concept of great client experience. As if you needed another reason for getting everyone on board with your brand ... or you needed another metaphor ... here it is for what it's worth. Let's look at this in two ways.

Anyone who has ever done the laundry has, on occasion, left a facial tissue or Kleenex in the pocket of a garment that is being laundered. That thin little piece of paper, about eight inches square in size, can have a surprising effect once the clothes are moved from the washer to the dryer. In the washer, the Kleenex pretty much stays in the pocket of the original garment. In the dryer, it breaks up and spreads all over every item of clothing. It is really stunning how much an eight-by-eight piece of three-ply, really thin paper can spread out to the whole load of laundry.

Making CARE a part of your brand requires the same thing. You need a small group of people who are willing to have their approach and skill set dealing with others get all over everyone else. In San Clemente surfer parlance, this is known as "sharing the stoke."

There is not one way to make this work. Every organization is different, and it follows that cultural change must necessarily follow different paths.

There is a basic to cultural change, and that is the capacity of human beings to change their ways if they so desire. The overarching concept is called neuroplasticity—the capacity of neural networks in the brain to rewire themselves. The brain is, according to *Brittanica.com*, quite an amazing organ. In this case, individuals who assert that they are hardwired to act in certain ways may be relieved to know that they can retrain themselves and re-hardwire their brains.

This, of course, won't be true for everyone. Some among the human race are so recalcitrant with respect to changing behavior that no amount of cajoling, training, rewarding, or talking can effect change. Perhaps the answer for those who don't like creating a great experience for your clients and refuse to change is some job behind the scenes or perhaps with another organization. Nevertheless, this step is focused on those who have the wherewithal to deliver what you ask of them, and those who have the desire to change and adapt to do the same.

Getting everyone to do what you want them to do is really the holy grail of business. Many companies have achieved this, and we've talked about several of them, like Apple, Nordstrom, and Tesla. This is where the second law of thermodynamics applies to the business world. There are, in fact three laws of thermodynamics, but I'll focus on the second law because it applies to this topic. This law is known as *entropy*. It asserts that all matter moves from order to disorder unless you apply energy to it. Simply put, you'll start off strong, but unless company leaders consistently apply energy to this cultural shift, it will swiftly move to disorder, at which point in time it becomes a former cultural shift.

The ideas presented herein have been successfully implemented—by work colleagues, friends who own small businesses, or my company. To be honest, mostly by others. They are worth trying if you think they fit your business. These are a way for you to continuously energize your brand of differentiated experience.

This involves understanding that sometimes a client will have a bad day and won't respond to anything an employee does. Sometimes an employee has a bad day and just can't get it right with a client. Have some grace for people, especially with your employees; this will energize them to try harder.

Hire for Cultural Fit

Perhaps this is the most reasonable and obvious approach. If you want your employees' personal brands to converge with your corporate brand, you need to hire people who have the attributes you seek. This may be the hardest thing to do, but it also may be the best thing you can do to get the right people in your organization.

You can give personality tests like Myers-Briggs. You can have unique and interesting interview situations to see how people operate within those situations. You can ask your existing staff who have the right personal brand if they have any friends looking for a job who have the right background, training, education, and personal brand. You can outsource this all to recruiters. You can hire people and carefully watch them over a six-month probationary period to see how they interact with your clients. Sure, any of these could work.

I'll give you some examples of hiring approaches that worked and some that didn't work.

Mark owns a small chain of coffee shops in Southern California. These shops are in coastal areas and have a very strong connection to the surfing communities in the beach towns where the shops are located. His whole brand revolves around a surf vibe. The shop in my town is always crowded, and if you spend any time there, you'll hear English being spoken in British, Australian, South African, Portuguese, and other accents. Surfers from around the world reside in this town because it has great year-round surfing spots.

This shop isn't exclusive to surfers. I'm not a surfer, and I like to go there. The interesting thing I observed was how the staff working in the shop, those taking orders and making the various coffee beverages, are just as friendly and polite to me (a nonsurfing, old dude) as they are to the hip young surfers with the killer accents. I always leave his coffee place feeling good about myself because I get treated in the same, friendly casual way that the staff treat their regular twenty-something, extraordinarily cool, surfing crowd. I wondered why, and I asked Mark if he did any special training.

Mark told me that he had developed a way to observe how people naturally interact with others and uses this as part of his hiring practice. When he has an open position, he brings a small group of potential employees into a room and then just leaves them in there. He watches them interact with each other. His goal is to find individuals with out-going personalities who, he believes, will be friendly and engaging to his customers—both the regular surfing crowd who are in there every day and others who may pop in from time to time.

Mark's business isn't the only one that uses this approach. Apple store employees have told me that Apple also tries to find people who already have strong interpersonal skills to hire for their stores. Apple believes they can train people to have the technical skills required to undertake their jobs. They provide lots of technical training, but, according to the store employees I've spoken with, they offer very little in the way of interpersonal skills training.

The online shoe company Zappos has a similar hiring approach. They want people who fit their culture of great customer service. They do a number of things with potential employees:

- Provide opportunities for the candidates to meet current employees in a social setting to see how they interact.
- Find out how they interacted or treated support staff. Many job candidates are flown to the Zappos home office for an interview.

Zappos will send a shuttle to collect them at the airport and return them to the airport. They'll ask the shuttle driver how they were treated by the candidate. If they were rude or dismissive to the shuttle driver, they won't get a job offer.

- After a week of training, Zappos offers their employees $3,000 to leave the company. People who buy in to the culture stay. Those who don't like the culture (Zappos said this is between 2 percent and 3 percent of their new hires) take the money and leave.

They are looking for polite, thoughtful, caring people who will be willing to go out of their way to create a great experience for their customers. Interestingly enough, when Zappos first starting doing this, their strategy was considered both innovative and risky. It seems to have worked well for them.

There are ways that don't work as well.

An executive in my company decided that we were not hiring people with the right personal brand and that the way to manage this was to ask each potential employee we interviewed to take a personality test to determine their work habits and personality traits relevant to the job. I was seeking to fill a midlevel position and was asked to trial this approach. Not knowing any better, I agreed to do this. I selected several people for phone interviews and found a candidate who I thought would fit the role. We brought the candidate to our home office for an interview, and I felt that his interview confirmed my initial reaction that he was a great person for the role.

Like a lot of companies, we have multiple people interview candidates, and all on the interview team agreed that this individual would be a great fit for our company. Also, like a lot of companies, we had to get final sign-off from my boss to put a formal offer in writing and send it to this candidate. My boss demurred. He refused to approve the offer letter. I inquired as to my boss's issue, if anything, with this candidate. I thought maybe he wanted to fill the position with some internal candidate who was interested.

My boss informed me that, based on the candidate's test results, the human resources team thought he would not be a hard worker and would not fit in with our culture. How could they have possibly drawn that conclusion? Not one HR person spent any appreciable time with this candidate. Even if they had spent hours speaking with him, how would they know that he would, or would not, be a hard worker?

There was a series of test questions around quality of life, hobbies, and what people do on the weekend, and the conclusion was that this individual preferred to spend time with his family or engaged in his hobbies in his nonwork hours and would therefore not be a hard worker. Of course he does. I think we all feel the same way about our time outside of normal business hours. I was stunned that they reached this conclusion.

There were no questions around what one would do if faced with a deadline to get a project delivered to a client. Had there been such a question, I have no doubt the candidate's response would be that they'd put the hours in to the project to get it delivered in a timely manner. I was unable to argue HR off of their perch, and we lost the candidate to a competitor.

The tests that are available are interesting but shouldn't be considered conclusive as to an individual's personality. I'll simply refer to my own Myers-Briggs test results, which are highly dependent on how I'm feeling that particular day, how much caffeine is in my system, and whether or not my favorite sports team won or lost the prior evening. I can take the test one day and be an extroverted leader, and the next time I take it, I turn out to be an introverted follower. It's very easy to change the outcome on these tests. Use them if you'd like, but be wary of the results.

There is a retail establishment that seems to hire people who want to help customers and simply brighten the customer's day. This is my local Costco in San Juan Capistrano, California. I don't know what they do or how they hire, but there are multiple employees who I feel have helped me, brightened my day, or just made the experience better. I don't personally know these folks, and I haven't been able to sit with them to better understand their story. I simply have observed how they act and how this makes those shopping at Costco react.

The first is a guy who usually is tugging around a cart of products or trash or some other stuff that he is moving from one place to another. He looks people in the eye and says, "Enjoy your Costco shopping experience." Let's break that down. Costco is definitely an experience, but it's often a negative experience due to crowds, checkout lines, or the fact that sometimes they don't have your favorite bagel chips in stock. That stinks. This guy is just trying to be positive, and I appreciate that. Maybe we should all be more positive.

The second is a woman who stands at the exit and checks your receipt. This is a big mystery to most of us. Why is she checking my receipt? Is she worried that I may be trying to sneak some merchandise out of the store without paying for it, or perhaps she's concerned that I've been charged for two sixty-count cases of French cookies when I am, in fact, only purchasing one. There's a reason for it, and Costco will tell you if you ask, but it is irrelevant to the actions of this individual. I noticed, one morning, an exit checker named Allison talking politely and positively to people. To the person directly in front of me, she said, "Nice to see you again," and he responded in some way that made me think they actually knew each other. I got up there, and she made some nice comment about my eyeglasses. I asked her if she did this for everyone, and she said that she did. It's just who she is. "Thanks for noticing my goofiness," she said to me. Nope, it's not goofy, Allison. It's very nice, and it makes for a better experience because you are making people feel good about themselves.

Finally, there's a person in the optical department named Marty. I had an issue with the fit of some sunglasses that I'd purchased over nine months prior. I was considering buying another pair of prescription sunglasses because I was tired of the wonkiness of my other pair. Mark was helping me and asked, "What happened to the sunglasses you just bought within the last nine months?" I took them out of my pocket and put them on. "Yeah," he said, "those are way off. I can fix them." Full disclosure, I'd been back two separate times to get someone in the optical department to fix them, and both times, the person did a half-baked job and told me, "This is the best I can do." Not Marty. He took the time, adjusted them several times, and ultimately, he manipulated them into the perfect fit. He saved me a lot of money, and I appreciate that.

Hiring people who seem to have the skills and personal brand you are looking for is perhaps the best way to build your brand. Most companies are already well established and have a lot of employees, and you obviously can't just replace them. Let's look at some other ways to shift to a client experience culture. I think the approach taken by Mark, Apple, Zappos, and maybe even Costco makes a lot of sense.

Training

You can train people to develop interpersonal skills, but this is hard to do, and simply put, not everyone will get there. Some people just are not good at making interpersonal interactions good for the client.

Training people for interpersonal skills ranges from minor touch-ups to doing a full personality transplant; sometimes transplants work, and sometimes they don't.

I led training sessions for client account managers in my company for three years. Many benefitted by this training and tried to share the stoke with their teams. In a disaggregated business such as ours, it's very hard to share client service concepts over the phone or simply to get people to both understand and undertake the CARE approach to service. There were no negative ramifications for those who cared to not use the CARE approach. As long as they met their performance metrics, executive management was cool with them giving their collective middle finger to the director of client service (that was me).

Our training sessions were supposed to combine work with fun. They were a bit of a grind—three nine-hour days in our training center in Colorado. The sessions were about trying to show the benefits of the CARE approach in multiple ways. I presented it to our team (pretty sure this was *not* the highlight of the three days). I engaged clients who came and talked about the value of experience and what experience meant to them. Company executives who had a long track record of creating great experiences for their clients came and shared their stories. I showed episodes of *The Office*. I liked the episode where Michael Scott wants to win back some clients by giving them gift baskets. We engaged the local improvisational theatre group to talk with us about flexibility and having an open mind. We went to the improv theatre, and they did a performance just for our group.

Some of our account managers were already there. They didn't need the training. They enjoyed hanging out in Colorado with their friends and hobnobbing with company executives.

Others saw the value of this framework. They adapted their approach and saw benefits such as year-over-year growth in revenues from their clients, additional opportunities to provide service to the client, and deepening relationships with key decision-makers in the client organizations. Those who were successful were able to get their entire team on board with the client service culture. Everyone serving that client was working within the CARE construct.

Companies do all kinds of training. I've gone through ethics training on an annual basis with three different organizations. At first, thinking that I'm an ethical person, I felt I didn't really need the training. I've taken a variety of sixty-minute-long ethics courses over the years. Going into these with an open mind, I usually pick up something that is of value to me. If you are going to do training, make it something that is reinforced on a periodic basis, just in case you have someone who needs to hear it three times before they believe it.

Set Broad Boundaries

Nordstrom is a retailer known for creating memorable, positive experiences for their clients. You may have heard the story about a Nordstrom employee accepting a set of four tires that were being "returned" one day. Nordstrom doesn't sell tires, as we all know, yet the clerk felt that they could accept this return, in that particular circumstance, on that particular day. There is definitely a backstory here; however, what is more important is that this clerk had the freedom to accept these tires because it was within the boundaries that Nordstrom had set for their employees.

Be careful with boundaries. Think about what it was like for you as a young teenager. You hated boundaries that were set by your parents. You also appreciated the boundaries because you knew how far you could go. Your employees may be the same way. They want the freedom to be themselves, but they also want to know where the boundary lines are. Boundaries should allow freedom for your employees within the necessities of your business.

This actual "returned tires" event (it really did happen, as recounted to me by a member of the Nordstrom family) provided an immeasurable amount of positive publicity for Nordstrom. It's still discussed today in business schools; I talk about it in my marketing class. It's the result of brand convergence and employees knowing how far they can actually go.

One way to look at this would be to tell employees to give the benefit of the doubt to clients. What does this actually mean in practice? The term *benefit of the doubt* was first used in the late eighteenth century in an Irish court. It meant that if the jury had some doubt with respect to the guilt of an individual, they were to accord that person the *benefit* of that doubt.

Since most retail establishments don't have juries that can help an employee sort through a client's story, what does this mean for your business interactions? It means you consider a client as honest and accept their story as true even if you have some doubts.

Just as an aside, some stories may come across as blatant falsehoods. The Nordstrom employee knew that they didn't sell tires. They also knew that in the recent past, there had been a tire shop at that location, from which the client purchased these tires, and they then gave the client the benefit of the doubt.

Back to the issue at hand. Set boundaries within which employees may make decisions that give your clients the benefit of the doubt. You know what these boundaries are for your business; find some set of employee-response boundaries that make sense for your operation.

The car rental company Avis offers another example of this. I'm a frequent renter, so they make it easier and easier to select a car, find that car when you arrive at your destination, get in it, and get out of the airport. I see that as a really positive experience, and it is, for me, consistently good. I've also had an instance where the Avis experience was crazy good because of the actions of one employee.

I was at a big industry conference in 1991 in San Francisco, and on the second evening of the conference, the Bay Area was hit by the Loma Prieta earthquake. The Bay Bridge was impassable due to a collapsed section. Local airports were reported to be closed. The people in my company huddled to try to figure out what to do, and one really clever senior executive got in line to use the pay phone to call the Avis 800 number and reserve three cars that we would pick up at six o'clock the following morning at their downtown San Francisco location.

The plan was to drive our team and any of our clients who wished to join us back to Southern California. This was a big earthquake. Buildings were damaged, and glass shards from broken windows littered the streets. A section of the Bay Bridge had collapsed, and we knew we'd have to find a way out of the city without knowing if any other major transportation thoroughfares were out of service.

There was no power. The city was lit by whatever starlight could make its way through the early-morning fog. We got up, got dressed, and miraculously found a cab to take us to the Avis office in downtown San Francisco, arriving there at 6:00 a.m., when they were scheduled to open. An Avis employee was there, and using flashlights and a ball point pen, he was able to manually complete the rental process.

He had no idea if we actually did have a reservation. We gave him a reservation number, and he gave us some options on cars. He did the old-school forms in writing, gave us a copy, and off we went. We collected our employees and clients, got out of the city, and made it that night to both Burbank and LAX, where people collected their own cars and got home.

Power was out, computers were down. This was pre-smartphone days. He did this all on paper forms using our Avis Wizard Numbers. Impressive—and memorable. Give people the right boundaries, and they will have the opportunities to create amazing experiences for your clients.

Talk About It

Cultural consistency requires three things. You have to deliver a *consistent* message that focuses on your culture; in this case, it focuses on creating great experiences for clients and how one may do that. You need to be *persistent*. Your consistent message needs to be delivered through multiple channels in multiple ways. Persistence means you aren't kidding around when you say you want everyone to create a great experience for clients. For those few employees who seem to struggle with the cultural concepts that you are talking about, you need to be *insistent*. You want everyone to be on board.

The "talk about it" approach requires that the big bosses talk about it. The big bosses being able to tell real stories about their approach to customer experience would be better. Nevertheless, if they don't talk about your CARE framework <u>and</u> demonstrate this to employees, no amount of talking will sway people to change their ways.

People operate at different tempos. Some will jump on board right away, and others may take a bit of time. For some account managers in my company, persistence was required. I have learned through experience that it often takes someone hearing a consistent message three or four times before it finally gets their attention. I had a colleague named Ray who, in my opinion, made contrariness part of his personal brand. As the marketing director, I often introduced new ideas or concepts that we could discuss with our clients. The idea was to keep clients abreast of new technologies that might be beneficial to them.

The first time I would talk with Ray about a new idea, he would say, "I have no idea what you're talking about." That can be deflating, but I decided to persist. A few weeks later, I brought up the same ideas to Ray, and he said, "That's very interesting, but I don't have any clients who would be interested." Giving it yet another try, I discussed this with Ray after another cooling-off period of about one month. His response was, "That's a great idea. Why didn't you tell me that the first time?"

Deliver a consistent message on the way you want your employees to create a great experience for your clients. Give them the information they need to create this experience. Provide them training if necessary. Don't deviate from your message. It should be the same on day three hundred that it was on day one.

Be persistent. Deliver it in multiple formats. Put it in daily briefings, monthly emails, and quarterly reports. Deliver it in training sessions, before you get on the bus with your team to go to a sporting event, on posters, on signs, any way you think will get to your employees and continuously remind them of your brand and your expectations for them to converge with your brand.

Finally, if you're the boss, you get to be insistent. You can insist that employees treat clients in the way that matches your brand of great experience. Perhaps you'll have to reassign someone who struggles with this to a position without significant client interaction Sometimes you have to let people go who aren't able to meet your expectations. If you have an employee who is not able to meet your requirements, you need to move them, or they'll stop the stoke—that's not good.

Have a System

A system is a way of doing things that you know can swing the odds of success in your favor. This could be a way of organizing your day, a system for dealing with irate clients, or a program for successfully executing repetitive work tasks. It's a way of doing things that results in success more often than not.

We just said that you should hire for cultural fit. Shouldn't that be enough? No, it's not enough. You have to give people a system for dealing with people.

Professional gamblers have systems. Gamblers who make a lot of money have very good, reliable systems. For the record, I'm not a gambler, but I'm fascinated by poker because the most successful poker players seem to be math geniuses coupled with an extraordinarily high level of emotional intelligence. They can assess the range of potential hands that their opponents have based on how the opponents are betting and their previous playing patterns. They can read their opponents, and they use these disparate data sets to calculate their odds of winning a hand. This enables them to make decisions with respect to folding, checking, and betting.

Sometimes their system doesn't work, and they are bested by a bluff or an opponent who simply gets very lucky and draws cards that help them beat the odds. Generally, if they follow their system and utilize their genius, good poker professionals can overcome the odds and win money in most of the tournaments they enter. Their system skews the odds in their favor.

Investors have systems. Lenders have systems. Salespeople have systems. These people have systems because their jobs involve people. Thus, their success in their jobs requires that they overcome the vagaries of human nature. Like the poker professional, great salespeople understand that they are dealing with people who don't always respond rationally. They don't have the Vulcan mind-melding powers of *Star Trek*'s Mr. Spock, so they can't always fully understand what is in someone's head. Their systems allow them some adaptability to adjust their thinking and response to unpredictable clients because not everyone makes their purchases solely based on logic (another one of Mr. Spock's signature traits).

Those of us who have jobs that involve people have jobs that also involve luck. That luck is manipulated in our favor through the use of a system. My company uses a system that was developed specifically for professional services firms, and it has proven to work the majority of the time. Our problem is that we don't always use this system because it takes time and effort. Often, we simply don't have enough time to fully execute the system, and we consign ourselves to uncontrolled luck.

Systems require effort. You must learn the system, learn how to use the system most effectively, and learn how to modulate the system based on inputs specific to your endeavor. Every great system leaves some flexibility for uncertainties and anomalies that may occur. To take advantage of this, you must be conversant in the details of the system, and you must have experience in using the system. Yes, this takes a fair bit of effort and time, but systems control the odds. You skew luck in your favor when you use systems that work and you use them as designed.

Systems skew luck in the aggregate. They change the odds, over time, in your favor. A great system does not guarantee success; you will still fail from time to time. A great system means your success rate is above average. You will see more success, and your increased success rate will be sustainable.

Zappos has a system. They have a way that they want their employees to treat their clients. Every new employee gets trained in this system by spending their first four weeks of employment working in the Zappos call center and learning how to respond to client needs using the Zappos system.

Systems take hold when you provide training for people. CARE could be your system for how you want your staff to create a great experience for your clients. If you don't like that, there are many consultants who will be happy to help you build a system, or you can develop your own system that works for your business. You need a system to give your employees guidance and guiderails for creating a great experience.

Get Close to Your Clients and Lead

General "Black Jack" Pershing took the American Expeditionary Force to France in 1918 to join the Allies in fighting the Axis countries in the Great War, now known as the First World War. He required his generals to join him at his headquarters in Chaumont. This was quite a distance from the front lines.

Every day, the commanding officers who were in the trenches would write down what had occurred in that day's fighting and send this summary via motorcycle courier back to Chaumont. The generals would then review the summary of the day's events, prepare orders for the following day, and send this back to the front lines via the same motorcycle couriers.

One of the American generals, Douglas MacArthur, stayed near the front lines rather than at Chaumont. He could observe what was happening in real time and make studied decisions based on his actual observations. His troops did much better than the troops that were taking orders from generals who were based in Chaumont and had never seen the front lines.

This isn't a history book, so why am I telling this story? It's the best metaphor I know for telling corporate leaders that they need to get out to the front lines so they know what is going on with their business.

Many executives actually do this. Airline executives will work on a cabin crew. Dara Khosrowshahi, the CEO of Uber, has gone out as an Uber driver to learn more about what it's like to be a driver and to hear directly from clients about their service. In my company, the CEO who influenced me the most (a fantastic leader named Murli) spent a lot of time with our company's biggest clients. He would often take extended trips around the world to see clients. He was the perfect person to do this. He has a great personality, is very knowledgeable of our company's capabilities, and has the ability to have tough discussions with clients in a very endearing way.

His goals were as follows: 1) get direct feedback, then deliver this feedback to engineering and construction teams so that we could improve our service, and 2) build relationships with these clients so that they would feel comfortable giving him performance feedback going forward. I learned from this, and in my operational management assignments, that is exactly what I tried to do.

Never walk alone. (These are lyrics from a song by Gerry and the Pacemakers as well as the song of the Liverpool Football Club in England.) If you are an executive going to meet with clients, you need to take people with you when you meet with clients. You should never walk alone. It's a training opportunity. I learned more by watching Murli in action with clients than I did going to any number of internal or external training sessions.

This aspect of leadership falls into the category of *servant leadership*. This term is attributed to a guy named Robert Greenleaf, who was the director of management development at AT&T in the middle of the twentieth century and published an essay titled "The Servant as a Leader." In this essay, Mr. Greenleaf lists his ten core principles of servant leadership that are fine, if a bit dated. Look them up; they are all excellent leadership attributes.

The servant leader has been around for thousands of years, not just a few decades. It is a model that has stood the test of time, although it has not always had the classy name bestowed upon it by Mr. Greenleaf. Servant leadership is a model that one can find when looking back through history. It has been demonstrated by business leaders, by many famous military leaders, and by even fewer politicians.

People will follow a leader who shows them that they are willing to roll up their sleeves and do the difficult things they require of their staff. There's no need to go into detail here; if you want people to follow, you have to lead.

Incentivize It

We all understand incentives. Bonuses, rewards, unexpected shout-outs in the weekly company emails. These are all part of the system. Do they work? Yes, they do—sort of.

Bonuses and rewards can become an expectation. Like Pavlov's dogs, we come running when we hear the tolling of the annual bonus bell. Once we get rewarded, we expect to get rewarded every time we do something great or every year when the annual bonuses are handed out. Can you imagine how frustrated Pavlov's puppies would be if they heard the dinner bell, came running to their master, and found out there was no dinner? That's what happens to your employees who have come to expect bonuses and rewards.

Exceptional service deserves a reward. A client called on one of our employees to fly to a project site in Alaska to help with a technical issue. This person took an overnight bag, got on plane, and came back thirty days later after the problem was fully resolved. He flew up there for three days and came back one month later. That's worth noting. That's worth rewarding because it is something exceptional. Someone provided exceptional service to a client. It was a great experience for the client, and the person was rewarded for their efforts. For this individual, I think one part of the reward was the satisfaction of fixing the problem to the client's satisfaction, but a monetary reward feels pretty good as well.

I'm not saying don't give bonuses and rewards. I'm saying think about their impact and use them appropriately, whatever that may mean for your organization.

One reward that I received always stuck with me. I was working with a colleague, Don, on a major proposal and presentation for one of the biggest projects that my company had ever pursued. Late nights and weekends were part of it. We were at it for two months. When the sales presentation was finalized, the senior VP for marketing came to us and told us to go out to dinner with our spouses, spend any amount we wanted, and put it on our expense report—he would approve it. We were surprised and elated; this was going to be good.

This was like a pipe dream to me and my wife. We had little kids at home, and a night out was rare. Even rarer was a night out at a fancy restaurant with no spending limit. We selected a nice French restaurant near our home, and upon being seated, we asked the waiter to select a bottle of wine for us. We had appetizers, entrees, dessert, wine, and dessert wine. The whole bill, in 1983, came to $125 with tax and tip.

We ate and drank ourselves under the table for $125—and with that small gesture, that marketing executive had my undying loyalty. If he needed something, I was there. I did several additional big proposals and presentations with that executive. All he had to do was ask. There were no more unlimited expense report dinners, but we were incentivized in other ways. I'd walk through a brick wall for that guy.

Ask Your Clients About It

Many companies rely on client surveys to see how their client-facing people are doing. Are these really the best way to get information?

We purchased a used BMW. The experience was fine. We negotiated a bit on price. The salesperson set us up with the dealer's finance person, who tried to upsell several different things to us, all of which we rejected. We finished the transaction after about two hours. It was now pretty late, and the salesperson invited us to return the following afternoon to get a tutorial on all of the technological features in the vehicle. We agreed on a time and returned the following day.

The friendly salesperson walked us through the various features on the car and was very patient with us. He did a nice job. At the conclusion of our business, the salesperson told us that we would be getting a survey via email and implored (I use this term as the midpoint between "ask" and "beg") us to give him all perfect scores ("Please give me tens on everything"), as his bonus was dependent on this.

What could the BMW dealer, or the salesperson, possibly learn from getting all perfect scores on the survey? He was fine. Nothing he did was amazing. Nothing he did was problematic. He was a good salesperson.

We aren't frequent car buyers, and, in fact, we've not purchased another BMW since that time. Do other customers come back to the same salesperson? Do they come back to the same car dealer every time they buy a car? Do they buy a new car every year or every other year? What was the purpose of the survey? Was it an implicit threat hanging over the salesperson's head, saying, "Treat these people right—or else"?

I don't remember how we scored the guy. I will say that if my wife did the survey response, he probably got all tens because she is a nice person. If I did the survey response, well, who knows?

Getting direct information from clients is a great idea, but what is the company really learning? What can they learn about client service and whether or not it was a great experience for that client? I think the best way to do this is to go face-to-face with clients. This was a car dealer, so it's hard to do that—or is it? They obviously had the time to try to get us to buy an extended warranty, so it's also likely that they could have asked us to answer a few quick questions from their client service manager at the conclusion of the transaction. They may actually have learned something if they had done so.

My company had a client service survey that they wanted to do. I was asked to provide ten clients to participate in the survey from my region, which I did. The intent was to either call the client to get them to answer questions or, if preferred by the client, send them an email with a survey they could then return to us. "Don't you want me to take this opportunity to go face-to-face with these clients?" I asked the survey manager. They told me that I could do that if I wanted to, but it wasn't necessary.

Every opportunity to go face-to-face with a client is not to be missed. I called and made appointments to visit with my clients, and I asked others on my team who were engaged in the survey to do the same thing.

One client I was particularly interested in speaking with was "Alan." He was at that time the city engineer for a local city with whom we were about one year into a multiyear engineering and construction effort. I called him up, made an appointment to get one hour of his time, and arrived at his office at the appointed time. He wanted to give me a tour of their new offices, and then he wanted to talk about some of his hobbies (skydiving was one of them, as I recall). I know the magic words to get someone to talk about something that they really like—"Please tell me more."

After about forty-five minutes of skydiving and heli-skiing talk, we turned to the survey. Immediately I sensed that Alan was being nice and not telling me everything. There was a problem, and it had to do with one or more people working on the project. I knew that because Alan, like most people, doesn't want to tattle on other people. I finally got him to open up and tell me the real problem. It wasn't a big deal, but it was bothering him, and we were able to fix it. If I had sent him the survey, we would have never known the issue, and it would have festered in Alan and may have caused us some problems down the road.

Surveys shouldn't be about an individual's bonus. They shouldn't be one-off efforts to get information that reflects one distinct point in time. They should be about finding ways to improve your clients' experience in dealing with your company. You should continuously be talking to clients to figure out how you can improve their experience.

You don't need a formal survey to ask your client questions. What could we do better? Are we meeting your expectations? What could we do to exceed your expectations? How can we make this a better experience for you?

Just ask. Most people will tell you, and some of the information you get may help you systematically improve your client experience offering.

The Big Client Experience Bus

We've talked about why client experience is a differentiator. We've discussed a framework called CARE that can help make your client's experiences with your company consistently better. Finally, we've offered some ways to get your people on the bus.

Lots of companies think they are really doing well. The executives see profits, growth, and potential. They see rising share prices, a big bonus, and their new ski chalet in Aspen as well.

They don't know if they are providing great experiences for their clients. Perhaps this concept doesn't merit discussion at corporate board meetings because it can't easily be boiled down to a series of numbers on a spreadsheet, fancy graphs that show growth trends or effect on shareholder value.

Client experience, in my experience, is a differentiator. The more pervasive the client experience concept becomes in your company, the more it stands out as a positive part of your brand.

Brands aren't spoken into existence. They are written down, to be sure. They are proudly spoken at company events. They are even used in promotional materials and advertising. All that is great, but a brand doesn't exist until it exists in the minds of your clients.

Brands don't get into your clients' heads through your promotional materials. Those help, but they are ephemeral because if your people, product, and service don't match your brand, then you aren't getting the right thing into the minds of your clients. Brands are supposed to evoke an emotional reaction in your clients' minds. Emotional reactions can be anywhere from great to awful; you want to stay on the great side of the spectrum.

Great client experiences are a powerful part of a company's brand that builds trust and loyalty in the minds of clients. It evokes powerful, positive, emotional reactions. It can build raving fans. It can propel companies to a leadership role in their sector. It can work for you!

ACKNOWLEDGMENTS

The creation of this book has not been a solo effort. It takes a village, and the villagers of my village contributed mightily. It starts with my wife, Connie, who read the first draft and gave me comments that fit into the hard truth category. She knows how much I appreciate her and love her. No one else could have done this.

Family is next. My four sons and their wives all contributed ideas and experience vignettes that were used as examples. I'm sure they got tired of my obsessive focus on client experience, but they never let on to that and humored me with some excellent examples of both positive and negative client experiences. One of my grandsons was also inspirational. You can correctly conclude that any references to a seven-year-old boy are references to this particular grandson who has just recently become brand aware and, in so doing, has developed some fierce brand loyalties.

My small but powerful posse of friends were also part of the journey. My great friend and fellow cyclist, Ryan, listened to me drone on ad nauseum about the book, which, in itself, was inspirational. Sometimes the most difficult thing is to just listen, and Ryan is world-class at this. Kurt, who is himself an author, read a beta version of the book and offered some fantastic ideas, all of which I took to heart. Mark, who is one of the owners of Sur Coffee (oft mentioned in the body of the text), let me talk about his great business, and when I showed him the sections that were written about Sur Coffee, he said the magic words, "That's awesome; I can't wait to read more." More powerful words have never been spoken to an author.

Many work colleagues contributed along the way. Fred, Don (both of them—you know who you are), Murli, Bobby, Harold, Christine,

Vicki, Ben, Paul, and many others. They provided inspiration and encouragement. From them I gleaned the inspiration for CARE, and with them I was able to turn this from an ethereal concept into a written product.

There were clients who, over the years, played a big role in the development of this approach. Gary, Brad, Harry, Bob, Lance, David, Steve, Jacob, Colin, Tim, and Jeff are just a few of them; it's a long list. We developed friendships as we worked together. I learned from them what it takes to create a great client experience and to win (and keep) the trust of a client.

Finally, many thanks to the team at Archway Publishing led by Bob DeGroff. Your professional and positive approach really made this book better.

Printed in the United States
by Baker & Taylor Publisher Services

Printed in the United States
by Baker & Taylor Publisher Services